CW00765953

Live Life

Sally Measom

Copyright © Sally Measom 2022

The moral right of Sally Measom to be identified as the author of this work has been asserted in accordance with the Copyright, Designs and Patents Act 1988.

All rights reserved. No part of this book may be reproduced or used in any manner whatsoever, including information storage and retrieval systems, or transmitted in any form or by any means, electronic, mechanical, photocopying, recording or otherwise, without the express written permission of the copyright owner, except in the case of brief quotations embodied in critical reviews and certain other non-commercial use permitted by copyright law. For permission requests, contact the author at the address below.

First edition printed by Mixam UK Ltd in the United Kingdom 2022.

A CIP catalogue record of this book is available from theBritish Library.

ISBN (Paperback): 978-1-7396167-0-0
Imprint: Independently published by one happy place.
Typeset design by Matthew J Bird

For further information about this book, please contact the author at:

www.onehappyplace.co.uk
sally@onehappyplace.co.uk

For my sons Daniel and James, my daughter Sophie, husband Craig and my mum.

Although my mum will never get to read this, I carry her courage, humour and love.

Contents

Contents [cont]

Contents [cont]

Live Life Your Way

You are never too old to set another goal or to dream a new dream
C. S. Lewis

We can all be limited by our past, childhood, trauma, school, learned behaviours, upbringing, friends, and the list goes on.

The good news is, you can press the reset button and change direction.

Take yourself out of the box, unwrap, and forensically examine, the good, the bad, and the ugly that is your life.

We are all unique, but the situations we find ourselves in are similar a lot of the time and we all experience a whole range of emotions, and that's not always easy to cope with.

When you question why you think the way you do, you can find out where your beliefs come from, then, you can start to understand how to change old patterns and think differently, moving towards a life you want to lead.

Simple exercises in this book will help you to question your reasoning, and the beliefs you hold about yourself and others.

You will discover practical ways to identify areas for change, using relatable experiences from my life to demonstrate the things that have helped me to move forward and think differently.

At the back of the book is space to write some positives, anything that resonates with you, the things you want to remember from the book, or thoughts the book triggers from experiences in your own life.

This is your time to start to Live Life Your Way.

PART 1

Perfect

Questions

Fitting In

If I distract myself enough, I won't have to deal with what's really going on

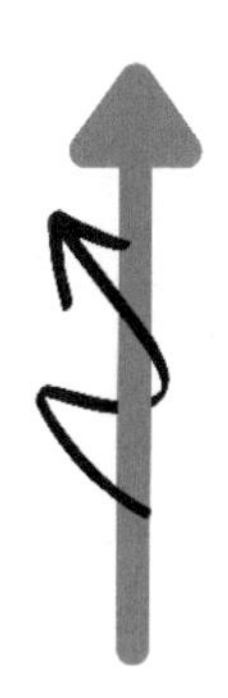

Perfect

Stop being perfect, because obsessing over being perfect stops you from growing
Brad Pitt

If you aim for perfection, you will always be disappointed.

There is no perfect, and the pressure to make this the norm is exhausting, to constantly strive for the impossible.

Whether it is your relationship, the way you look, how your children behave, what you achieve at work, or how compatible and successful your partner is, nothing is perfect.

The cost of trying to be perfect and being everything to everyone at the expense of yourself is too high.

If you do the best that you can at the time, juggling all the different parts of your life and the pressure that brings, and you end up with a scorecard marked "good," then you are doing well.

Take the pressure off yourself and others to be perfect.

We often try to be perfect because we have a sense of our inadequacy and feel that we don't measure up.

The need to be perfect often relates to messages we received during childhood. Maybe from a parent or a teacher at school, messages that we were not good enough, that's how we received them anyway.

Perhaps they weren't intended to come across this way, random comments that have affected us negatively for years.

So, we understand that the only way to not receive further criticism is by being perfect. Stifling our growth and creativity in the process as now we operate within safe boundaries and conform.

By taking control of your behaviour, making things simpler, and being present in the moment, you will give yourself the best chance to enjoy your life.

Focusing on what is important and fulfilling will help to make you happier in the long term, trying to reach unattainable standards will not.

This means dealing with all the things that stop you from doing that and designing the life you want to lead with the people you want in it.

Questions

The biggest adventure you can take - is to live the life of your dreams
Oprah Winfrey

I am a runner, not a quick one, and I have a very competitive nature, so I was constantly disappointed with my times and my performance.

Running is part of what I do in my leisure time, it keeps me fit, lets me drink wine, and gives me time to think. Yet, I felt that I should be controlled and constrained by a watch as if the only important part of my running was the achievement of a specific number.

I took off the watch and focused on the feeling and achievement of just running.

Being there in the moment, taking notice of what was around me, looking at the world, and enjoying it.

I use it now as my creative time, usually just me and my thoughts.

This has helped to unlock a part of my brain and personality that had been well hidden for many years, my creative side.

I just needed to give my brain time to stop and explore what else might be out there in the world for me.

I now try lots of different things. I am having abstract art classes, which are joyful. They allow me to become completely absorbed, playing at it like a child would, with no embarrassment or judgement, it's so much fun and has enhanced my life in so many ways.

If you can try new things with no preconceived ideas and go into it with an open mind, you will find new worlds that you can become a part of, and some of these will change your life.

Things that were alien to me only a few years ago are now a regular part of my life as I tried and liked them, and they are good for me both mentally and physically.

When I started outdoor swimming two years ago, I met a new friend who is now one of my best friends.

It was such a surprise to me, to make such a strong friendship and have an instant bond like this.

The ridiculousness of what we were doing, combined with the way we looked in woolly hats and swimming costumes, on the banks of a local river, made us smile.

We felt silly and a bit vulnerable, but we acknowledged and embraced the feelings together, giggled, got in and we have never looked back.

I should add that now we don't care what we look like, if we get in at the wrong place or if we scream from the cold water, we use this as our playtime.

I have limited education, and my highest qualification is from college.

At times in my career, I have been tempted to invent a university education just to be able to fit in and join a conversation.

When people say that they have come from the school of life, we all have, the usual nature v nurture debate is interesting.

Our genetics tumble from one generation to another, but I am more focused on choosing to live the life I want to live now, looking at what I am spending my time on, and what might be stopping me from living that life.

Now is the time for you to do the same in your life.

How you translate your experiences into your everyday life, and what you place importance on as an individual and overall, as a society, is interesting.

How we let this define us and how we then choose to move forward makes all the difference.

I recently heard the phrase, "Death is the background noise whilst life carries on around us" with this in mind we need to start living.

So, some questions to contemplate as we begin -

If you could have absolutely anything and you had no limits with money or responsibilities, just the freedom to choose, what would it be?

How would your life look?

Think about what you want from your life with very big picture thinking for now.

Starting in a no holds barred big picture way allows you the freedom to explore.

Although you know it's unlikely that the big picture will become your reality, when you scale it back and start looking at the smaller details in your life, some changes seem more possible.

You can start to review what you want, and how you can put steps in place to get there.

It doesn't feel as hard to think about when you give yourself permission to just start.

More questions -

Could you make some sort of plan for your future to make you healthier and happier?

Could this plan take you forward toward your goals, and might this plan also help you to cope when things get tough?

Your plans will be personal to you and the good news is that you are the expert in your own life, and with a bit of practice you can write a plan and then actually start to achieve it.

It is likely that your plan will encompass your personal and professional dreams and aspirations no matter what size they are.

You will use it to drive you towards setting your goals, giving you the best chance of success, and helping you to build some resilience in your life.

Finally -

Why do some of us keep doing things that ultimately make us unhappy?

It's an interesting question and I suspect a lot of us choose not to move forward because of our self-worth, confidence issues, fear, or perhaps you take comfort in what is familiar.

You know that change is hard and involves some risk but if you want it enough the choice to change is yours to make.

As you think about what you want from life, and how you can actively plan your future, you will learn that you can choose change as a positive option in your life.

Fitting In

Fitting in is boring. But it takes you nearly your whole life to work that out
Clare Balding

Throughout most of my childhood and through the rest of the 80s, I created a chameleon-like character for myself, and I managed to fit in almost anywhere, this could explain why I am so good at sales.

It could also explain why it took me so long to find out where I fit. When I could stop trying to prove to others that just being me was enough once I found my kind of people, my true values, and who I felt most comfortable with.

Throughout my school years, I wasn't particularly happy or unhappy.

I was always impatient to get to the next stage of my life, particularly being able to drive and leave home, so that in my eyes, my life could finally begin.

Highlights at school, because it wasn't all bad, included anything to do with drama and school plays, playing someone else and being absorbed in a different world was very liberating for me, as I happily escaped from reality.

Looking back at my diaries from that time, my obsession with comprehensive note-taking extended to my latest boyfriend and my social life, unfortunately, I was not as diligent when it came to my studies.

I was like most teenagers I know, appearing blusteringly confident while demanding attention, when actually, I had little confidence, was completely consumed by how I looked and was desperate for the approval of others.

Jump forward to having my children, two boys and a girl, and I have seen first-hand this need for approval a lot more in my daughter than I did in my sons, but that's just my experience.

The peer pressure to conform and fit in is huge, with little acceptance or celebration of any difference or uniqueness both mentally and physically.

So, if you are very bright and love maths it is often frowned upon, so you hide it.

If you look different from what is currently fashionable in any way you are considered odd.

When I was at school a slim figure was fashionable, and I had quite big hips and legs so was taunted with the occasional nickname of thunder thighs.

My daughter is currently at school and the fashion is for big legs and a big bum. I was born at the wrong time.

I think this illustrates how ridiculous judging someone on the shape of their body is.

Trying to conform to the stereotype of what is acceptable means that you make bad decisions to be part of the crowd.

The feeling of freedom that comes with understanding that you can't control what other people say and what they think of you, no matter how hard you try, is refreshing.

My eldest son had learnt a new word at nursery school and chose to use it when he was waiting with his gran at a busy bus stop.

I am not sure the assembled pensioners were ready for the word "fuck!" at 8 am from my four-year-old.

My point is that people will do and say what they want, and no amount of worrying will change this.

Understanding that taking care of yourself is the most important thing, it allows you to be the human being that you want to be, and changes not only your world but the world for those around you.

Being true to yourself and choosing not to follow the crowd can be difficult and unpopular.

You will make other people question their choices and this will make them uncomfortable, which can result in mean and defensive behaviour.

When you are younger, I think this is particularly difficult as you want to feel that you are part of something and that your tribal needs are met by the acceptance of others.

The pool of people you meet in your everyday life may be quite limited and the need to fit in very strong.

When the primitive need to belong is strong, ask yourself how much of you are you having to sacrifice to fit in?

If the answer is too much, think again about your worth, your value and uniqueness, and realise that this time in your life will pass.

Although it is horrible, you will not be in this position with these people forever.

We have all come from different places with unique backgrounds and experiences and you can't change that, but, if you delve into new experiences, people, and places, then deep within yourself your limiting belief patterns will start to change along with your outlook on life.

Ultimately your future will change as you start to open yourself up to all the things that might be possible in your life.

This is when you start to experience life your way, as you get to design and shape your future into one you want to get out of bed for. Your life then becomes less of an accident, and you have more of a plan.

F#@K
Bus
Stop
What did
he say?

If I distract myself enough, I won't have to deal with what's really going on!

Life is so much easier when you don't hoard your past
Adele

If we keep doing up houses, planning the next building project or house move and I project manage everything, I will be fine emotionally as I won't have time to think about anything.

This was me; it is what I did to avoid dealing with anything that was emotionally too difficult, specifically my marriage.

You might be busying yourself in other ways to avoid dealing with situations in your life. In my case, I didn't realise this was what I had been doing for years until a long time afterwards, it was my version of running away.

This relates to my first marriage, where we paid no attention to the needs of the other person but stayed on one common path.

Both treading familiar ground, united towards the next extension or a bigger house, as if this was enough to sustain a healthy, happy relationship. Let alone the question of some sort of work-life balance, with our shallow measure of success only being measured materially.

The distraction technique is an effective way of avoiding the things in life that you know are not right and need dealing with.

You start to do more and more, convincing yourself that you are too busy right now to deal with anything else.

It doesn't have to be as drastic as building and moving house. It is anything you do that enables you to shut your emotions down, to disconnect from the underlying unhappiness that you know is there.

Not being able to look at and connect with the past, present, and future and deal with your unhappiness is disastrous and eventually, something will have to give.

You cannot live a happy and healthy life if you are not able to be honest with what you want and need from it.

If this is you, start slowly, identify what you are avoiding, and take your time to think through what would happen if ...?

Put yourself in all the possible scenarios if you made a change.

Think how each new scenario you'd find yourself in would meet your needs, the ones you have become so good at hiding.

If you continue to avoid meeting your needs, it can lead to anxiety and obsessive behaviour with constant stress.

It is destructive to keep squashing your inner voice, the one that warns you that something fundamental isn't right. If you refuse to listen it creates inner turmoil and it's exhausting.

In my case, I subconsciously added a glossy pretentious sheen to my outer self which helped me to build a solid wall between how I appeared to others and how I felt inside.

It was like living with two different people in my head, not a great place to be.

It took me years to realise what I had been doing, to learn this lesson, and to understand that being busy all the time means that I am avoiding dealing with uncomfortable truths.

Finally letting go of my marriage and the future path it was leading me down, gave me the time and space to reflect, listen to my inner voice and discover myself again.

PART 2

Change

You can't be good at everything, but you can learn to be better

Belief systems

Belief in yourself

Labels

Change

The only one thing that is constant is change
Heraclitus

Change can be hard; it is more comfortable for us to do what we have always done as it's familiar and feels safer.

That doesn't mean it is good for you to keep doing the same things over and over, never challenging yourself or moving forward in your life.

I have found that choosing to change something is worth it most of the time.

If you get it wrong sometimes, at least you will have learnt from the process.

Trying something new, maybe a different style of clothing, a new hairstyle or activity, seeing yourself, and letting others see you in a new way, allows you to begin to rewrite the script of your life.

You might enjoy playing another role, redesigning yourself and seeing how it feels.

Who says you must always be the way you are right now?

If you are very happy with everything in your life you are probably not reading this book. If changing superficial things like clothing, hair, or taking up a new activity is not for you, and you want more fundamental life changes then think about what you want out of your life.

If you write it down, it's helpful and makes you accountable.

Setting some life goals with time frames in mind will lead you to success, we will go through this in more detail later in the book.

Starting small, with one change at a time, ticking it off and congratulating yourself when you achieve the change, before moving onto your next goal becomes a lifelong habit with practice.

You will work out how to deal with the feelings you have when dealing with problems and confrontation, thinking more about what you say and how you respond to others.

If a question or situation keeps playing on your mind, you will be able to review, question and understand why, and learn how you can move on from it.

You won't be needing to ask the audience (friends, family members, colleagues) for their opinion until you are confident about what you want to change, and you may not need to consult them at all.

Well-meaning people may not be ready for the changes you want to make in your life or be supportive when they understand how it might affect them.

By changing the way you behave and react, the dynamics of your situation will change and so will the outcome.

We will also look at how understanding personality types better can help with this.

I am not surprised by how much we inevitably alter throughout our lives, we have always been different versions. If you think about the version of you when you were young and out with your friends versus you at home with your parents, they are likely to have been quite different.

Using vastly alternative language in each situation, changing your behaviour depending on your mood.

We learn to fit in and fall out along the way, sometimes the life and soul of the party at other times we disappear under the radar in search of a quieter life.

You are continually bombarded with new things, taking on new experiences, from being a single person to part of a couple, then maybe becoming a parent, perhaps dealing with illness or death, not to mention job changes.

It is no surprise that these changes turn you into alternative versions of yourself and some of the changes will be harder to cope with than you imagined.

Combine these life events with questions of self-doubt and self-worth. Throw in your genetic mix and the type of upbringing you had, and you have a colossal number of factors that come into play before you make any decision, good or bad.

The conscious and subconscious behavioural choices you make in each situation are fuelled by something that is going on inside you.

This is possibly driven by a fear of failure, being desperate to fit in or not wanting to be alone.

Perhaps you act in risky and random ways trying to impress the crowd or withdraw completely from social events. Remember you own your actions, they are still directed by versions of you. We will look at why you behave in this way and where your thinking comes from.

If you don't like who you are, you can always change into someone you like much better. We will unpick the long-held beliefs you hold about yourself to help with this process.

You are a unique mixing pot of a human being and confusion and indecision come as standard for most of us.

If you are not in the place you want to be, with the people you want alongside you, we will look at the steps you can take to gain control and change these parts of your life.

Changing small things builds the confidence to move on to changing the big scary stuff.

It helps you to make better decisions and become the director in the story of your life, heading in the direction that you want to go, living a fulfilling and more purposeful life. Basically, life becomes less of something that just happens to you when you actively take your place in the driving seat.

You can't be good at everything, but you can learn to be better

Success is loving life and daring to live it
Maya Angelou

Although I am good at a lot of things, my mind is constantly solution-driven, this is not great if all you want from me like my husband, friend, or children, is a bit of understanding and empathy.

I try to solve everything, always trying to find an answer in every situation. I have had to learn to step back, reflect and sympathise sometimes.

If you recognise this behaviour, it's an important lesson in learning to listen. Actively listen, and respectfully hear what someone else is trying to tell you, not just waiting for a pause in the conversation so you can speak to get your point across.

If you think this might be you, take notice of how often you interrupt someone when they are speaking, before they have gathered all their thoughts and finished what they wanted to say.

Try to stop constantly rehearsing what you want to say in your head before you speak.

You can't properly listen without fully emptying your mind, opening your ears and holding back to give the other person their deserved audience.

I have learned to be much more emotionally intelligent as I have experienced different situations in life.

I make sure that I read a wide variety of books, some I don't like at all to start with, an unfamiliar genre can be challenging, but persevering is worth it to expand your mind.

Listening to and learning from other great people is a smart thing to do.

People don't necessarily know better than you, they might just know different things that they can share to help you, so you can learn from experiences they have had in their life.

I am impatient which is good and bad. It gets things done but is frustrating for me and everyone around me when things are not moving forward fast enough, personally and professionally.

I have learnt that sometimes the right thing to do is nothing for now, to stop, wait and let things play out, and see what happens.

If you recognise yourself in this, it is helpful to realise that we all move at our own pace. Dancing to our tune and moving at our speed, and no amount of shouting, cajoling or tantrum-type behaviour will result in other people behaving in the way you want them to, or at your unachievably sustainable speed.

The wise ones have decided a long time ago that the whirlwind of chaos with which you surround yourself will not be for them, as they have already chosen a calmer path. They get there in the end, less ruffled and with lower blood pressure.

I am good at stripping things back and making them simple which is good in a business sense, I like to plough a clear path through all unnecessary complic-ations.

This is so useful when planning your life as often the overwhelming amount of daily, weekly, and monthly tasks means that you decide not to start any sort of planning in the first place. Looking at your priorities becomes vitally important to move forward.

I am obsessive, I want to get things right and can repeat problems over and over in my mind and out loud, to the point where I am nearly driving myself and others mad.

Who doesn't have a problem sitting in their mind that churns around as you search for an eject button to escape from it?

Taking on those problems, rationally dealing with them, and allowing yourself time to process the results of your actions, or your choice of inaction is something you must find time for.

I have learnt to laugh at myself more as I get older and realise that very little matters in the long term, knowing that if I leave a job for whatever reason, someone else will quickly take my place.

Everything moves on, change is inevitable, and we need to relearn how to enjoy the now.

As young children we live from moment to moment completely absorbed in our task, unable to grasp much beyond our immediate world, when does this change?

I'm not sure on which day we all decide that we are grown up now.

Do we decide before society chooses for us what is childish and needs to be left behind?

It's such a shame when we stop doing something that gave us so much joy.

Why do we stop doing it and replace our life with a lot of complicated rules and behaviours that constrain us and make us unhappy?

I know it is time to start to learn again with a mind open to all possibilities, to rediscover your childlike wonder within the world. To do this successfully you will need to remove some of your mental and possibly physical clutter in the process.

Belief systems

A belief system is nothing more than a thought you've thought over and over again
Wayne W. Dyer

What do your belief systems say about you and where does your thinking come from? Your belief system is developed based on your history and the experiences that you have had in your life, and this can be very limiting.

It is useful to question your thoughts and beliefs regularly.

If you imagine that each fixed belief is in its own box, take it out and examine it with all the associations and negativity that surround it to see if it is still true, or was ever true in the first place.

It could be related to happiness, food, health, relationships anything where your limiting emotional thoughts and beliefs can trap you into believing it is true.

Beliefs about yourself like, "I have never been able to make friends," need a little unpicking and more thought, it is very unlikely to be true.

Although you might completely believe it, causing you to act in a way that makes this true.

Maybe you believe you will never be confident in a big group of people.

Again, this is not a fact just your belief, so challenge your thinking behind this statement.

Don't let yourself get away with avoiding trying something you can learn to be better at, it just needs to become more familiar and that will happen with practice.

It could be something quite big, like travelling on a plane or going abroad for the first time, it could be a small step, but it seems very big to you, maybe meeting a new friend for coffee.

You know what you avoid doing, but would like to try, and how you convince yourself that it is not for you.

It doesn't fit with your limiting beliefs, you will panic, you'll look stupid, you are bound to fail, it hasn't worked before, the list of excuses for you not to try goes on and on.

I believed for a long time, about 40 years if I am honest, that I was not creative, having failed my Art O level at school, I honestly thought the field of creativity was solely defined by being able to draw.

I realise that this sounds naïve now, but it was only when someone at work mentioned that I always creatively problem solved that the penny finally dropped, and I realised that I have been creative all my life.

That one comment from my colleague gave me the confidence to question, look at and then laugh at my belief system.

As I looked back over the years, I have always been creative.

I have sung in a band, acted, presented, and solved problems all my life.

I presumed I wasn't creative as this was what I was told in childhood.

I now know that this isn't the case, it's not a fact, and I shouldn't have believed it for so many years.

The narrative that played in my head was incorrect, I had to change it and no longer let it be my truth.

It did hold me back, not in an earth-shattering way, but I had already decided that I couldn't do a lot of creative activities and didn't want to try, as I presumed I would be no good at them.

Not being good at something I now know is ok, but in my quest to be brilliant at everything I sadly used to limit myself to only those activities that I had some success in.

I am actively making up for the lost time in every creative way possible, and you can challenge your beliefs in just the same way.

Look closely at those beliefs you hang onto, and question if they are true.

Is it easier to keep believing them than confront them?

You might be able to quash them once and for all when you establish that they restrict you in your life. Challenge them, acknowledge them but don't let them win.

I now talk to my mind along the lines of "thank you for bringing that to my attention, but that belief is no longer true/was never actually a fact" and I move on and prove how right I am as I demonstrate my new truth to myself.

In my home life, it was made clear that no one in my family was very good at maths, so the expectation was low. I went into my maths classes knowing that I wouldn't be able to do well.

Guess what, I followed the anticipated route and failed maths.

However once at college and out into the wider business world, I discovered that I am very capable with numbers. I just needed to believe it and find a way to learn that suited me.

It is frightening how much you miss out on because of the limits you impose on yourself.

I have tried very hard not to impose limiting beliefs upon my children.

Although I know that we often do it to ourselves with self-deprecating humour, before a parent, brother or sister unhelpfully sets that belief in our mind.

If you are in danger of believing that facts are involved, you should know that this is rarely the case.

It is more likely that history says that you have always thought this way and believed these things so this is what you must keep doing.

Unless you open your mind to question how and why you think the way you do, you will trundle through life missing out on people, places and new experiences that you would enjoy.

Fear is another limiting factor when you try to protect yourself or when others have been very over-protective.

All you see is danger in every new situation and you believe it is lurking around every corner.

You convince yourself that it is not safe, and you might get physically or emotionally hurt. This might be a rational fear, deeply ingrained, rightly trying to protect you if you are about to jump out of a plane.

For most of us in everyday life, it can stop you from changing that job to pursue what you really want to do, or taking a chance on that new relationship, because your belief system says the risk of getting hurt or getting it wrong is too high.

If you can adjust your thinking after challenging yourself to question your beliefs, you can move forward and start to imprint some new less limiting, more positive beliefs into your mind.

As you successfully start to navigate your way through a lot of new experiences that don't kill you and you find you enjoy, they can fulfil a need that you may not have realised was there.

How others see you throughout this process as you expand your horizons can be positive and negative, some people will feel that you are leaving them behind, but they are free to challenge themselves and move forward.

Please don't be limited by what someone else says you can and cannot do.

This is a moment to trust yourself, take your courage in your hands, remember to breathe, and imagine yourself succeeding at something you have always wanted to try, no matter how small, then go and do it.

Start your new adventure now.

Belief in yourself

You are braver than you think, more talented than you know, and capable of more than you imagine
Unknown

It is easier when someone believes in you and can guide and coach you well from the beginning, maybe your parents or grandparents, people who are well and truly on your team.

Building belief in yourself and being confident takes practice for most of us. If we have some good experiences, alongside people who care and pick us up when we fall, we have a much better chance of success.

When I started my career in hospitality, two people said I wasn't good enough and wouldn't make it as a manager.

I tried hard to impress these people and thought I was doing a good job. Neither approached me to help, guide or coach me in my job or offer any support.

At 18, I didn't understand why I felt so isolated.

Fortunately, I then had an area manager who saw potential and helped me to understand how I could improve. Simply by talking to me and explaining how I could relate to my team better, learning to work together with them.

I clearly remember him asking me what I would do, if I asked a member of my team to do something, and the team member thought they knew a better way of doing it than me.

My answer was that I would make them do it my way, I was in charge, and they should listen to me.

He replied, "What if their way was better?"

I learned that a title doesn't mean a lot.

If you are not listening to your team, neither you nor your team will ever reach its full potential.

Success is never a one-man show.

Belief in yourself shouldn't be limited to the approval of others, but someone in your corner helps as you try to establish yourself in a new way.

I also learnt that in a family situation, it is damaging to your children when you are not listening to them.

It is easy to get distracted with many other tasks appearing as priorities.

When you actively listen and ask questions without dismissing their viewpoints and opinions, you help to develop confident children with well-thought-out ideas.

In a much later job, I struggled to work out where I fitted in, as I successfully took the working together principle forward throughout my career. Unfortunately, I was back to being directed to work confined within my department, working separately from the rest of the business. I knew my way of working was better and I fought hard for the whole business to work together as one big team.

My past experiences and the insight gained in my earlier roles meant that my instinct was right.

I had the confidence to speak up, and the business grew with the changes made as I had previously developed the belief in my ability.

Championing others and helping them to shine and grow, has become more important to me than having a big career now.

If you need more confidence and help to develop at work, school, or university, try to find a trusted advisor who will have your best interests at heart.

If this isn't someone at home, look further afield to find the right person.

We are all learning all the time and if you haven't done something before how are you supposed to know how to do it?

Don't be afraid to ask for help, if whoever you ask makes you feel small, find a different person, it says more about them than you.

I have been into many businesses as a business consultant and communication is the number one issue.

I am often told that everyone knows the plan and understands the business, it communicates well.

As I scratch the surface and talk to team members at all levels this rarely proves to be the case.

It is destabilising for everyone and does not breed a culture of self-believers who are confident to make decisions as everyone tries to hide under the radar not sure what will happen next.

Building great relationships and having a clear plan are key requirements, so you know which direction you are all heading in, enabling you to work together to get there.

A good company like a good parent should be interested in investing in you so that you can believe in yourself.

How you run your life personally is very like running a business.

Communicating daily with your partner and friends instead of your colleagues or customers and building your relationships with those inside your circle and those on the outer edges of your life.

If you take control of your work and home life with a plan, this guides you onto the next part of your journey.

Sometimes a happy accident makes you change direction or takes you off course, but that's ok you can adjust the plan.

Belief in yourself helps you to move through life's unpredictable changes and gives you the confidence to live your plan.

A word of caution, you are programmed for it not to be that easy.

As I have said previously your belief system is often flawed, as your stored emotional memories affect how you react to a situation.

You are pre-programmed to react based on your belief system, it doesn't consider your rational mind when it decides anything, it immediately knows how it feels about a change of any kind.

Therefore, you must consciously consider your belief system to explain your thinking and your behaviour to understand how to change it.

For example, if I have been hurt in the past by an unfaithful partner my belief system may say to me that I will always be hurt in the future, it is an emotional response directly from my belief system.

So, when the person who might be the perfect new partner for me comes into my life, the way I react because of my belief system means that my belief system is in charge and wins before any discussion to the contrary can take place.

It is running my life, so it will never let me move forward and take a chance on this new person.

Although my rational mind would say that being hurt once does not mean I will be hurt by everyone for the rest of my life, it doesn't get a look in because my belief system isn't listening.

When you become aware of why your belief system works the way it does, and where your reactions come from, you can trace the root cause back often many years.

Then you can reprogramme yourself to start to overcome your hesitation and fear.

By consciously questioning and changing your internal responses, moving on to fact and reality-based decisions in the future, your belief in yourself will change, and you can start to direct your own life again.

Identify the top 3 limiting beliefs that you have about yourself and see if you can unpick where they came from, then challenge them loudly.

Now write down 3 people who have believed in you, and who had or continue to have a positive influence in your life.

Those people who selflessly helped you to believe in yourself and shaped you into who you are today.

Use them as your inspiration for moving forward and pass on the gift of encouragement and support to others.

Labels

You can't complain about being labelled angry if you make angry comments
Brian Nick

I am a mother to 3 children, a wife, a friend, a parent to a dog and a cat, a runner, an outdoor swimmer, a presenter, a salesperson, a writer, an amateur artist, self-employed, impatient, enthusiastic, chatty, persistent, and much more.

We are all defined by the labels that we are given.

Some are forced upon us, whether it is just a plain fact, or an opinion we have of ourselves. Maybe it's a label given to us by others, a character trait that they have seized upon and labelled you with.

Think about what defines you, your uniqueness.

What do you stand for and believe in, who are you and who would you like to become?

Don't let yourself be limited by a title or a label and the character traits that other people always expect from you.

In the same way that you understand that your belief system can be very fixed and you need to challenge it, being labelled is still trying to fit you into a specific box for convenience.

It is more comfortable and familiar for other people to be able to define and describe you easily.

If you want to make a positive change, be the exact opposite of one of your expected traits.

If you are known as the difficult younger sister stop playing that role and act differently.

If you and others think you have never been good at sport and this has become your truth, challenge this label.

According to Google, there are over 8,000 indigenous sports and sporting games, you can't have tried and been bad at all of them.

I am being flippant but trying to illustrate how to not write yourself off, or write off what you could add to your life in the process.

I know people who drive me crazy when they say they don't like vegetables.

Again, thanks to Google, I can tell you that at the last count there are 1,097 species, so trying a few more must be an option?

You can reinvent yourself any way you want.

It might feel awkward and a bit strange at first, but in no time, friends, colleagues, and family will start to see you differently.

They will have to adjust their thinking to accommodate the new you, creating new labels for you in the process.

PART 3

The power of 3

What do I want to do?

Different personality types

Management at any level, being one or being managed by one

Better business

First impressions

Presenting

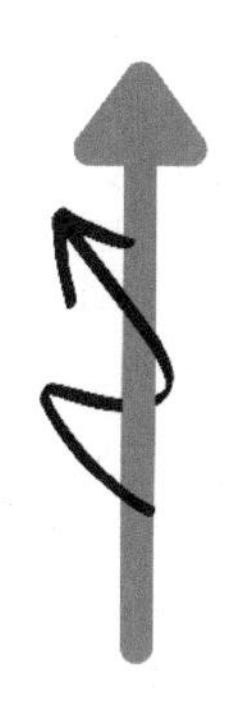

The power of 3

Three is my magic number!
Sally Measom

Apparently, your short-term memory can only hold about 7 separate items at any one time, depending on the individual.

I seem to be capable of choosing and effectively achieving 3 things at a time and only if I write them down.

The power and effectiveness of using 3 is well tried and tested in the presentation, advertising and marketing world as being the most powerful and impactful way to get a message across and make it stick.

Either saying the same word three times or highlighting a point using three related phrases or statements mean that the message is clearer, more persuasive and you are more likely to remember it.

I have worked in many jobs, own my own business, and have worked for a large company as a director. I know that the further up the corporate ladder you go the more complicated we seem to make things for no good reason.

Huge lists that we never get to the end of, massive chunks of time and money spent at planning sessions to come up with too many ideas to not implement or move forward on any of them.

This can be true in your personal life as well, with so many priorities competing for your time, and an overwhelming number of tasks it is hard to know where to start, so you don't start at all.

I use the simplicity of reducing everything in my life into 3 to help me focus and plan.

Starting with the big things that keep going around in your head, the things you keep coming back to, maybe they are keeping you awake at night.

You never really find peace with them as they seem too huge, start by dealing with just 3 of them.

Break your thinking down into 3 main headings.

If you write down 3 clearly defined and achievable headings, give yourself only 3 main things to think about this week, you will have focused your thinking, and be ready to convert your priorities into action.

Now for each main heading add a subgroup of 3.

It is an effective way to make yourself move forward and get things done.

It is not complicated it just takes a bit of practice to distil your thinking down to just 3.

I find that if you don't put in a specific subgroup of 3 for each main heading, you think too widely. The random nature of thinking too widely gives you too many alternatives about where to start.

This doesn't result in the focus and action you need to start moving forward.

An example of my planning from a few years ago looks like this –

Main 3	**Sub 3**
Children	Support GCSEs (youngest child)
	Support Uni (middle child)
	All, mental health, and wellbeing
Work	Current job (I was unhappy and wanted to move jobs)
	Future job
	Work-life balance (I wanted more leisure time)
Partner	Our wedding (postponed due to lockdown 3 times)
	His business (challenges after lockdown)
	Holidays (when and where?)

All big things that needed my time and attention, 3 main priorities, with 3 sub-groups, linked strands telling me what specifically about, children, work and partner I needed to focus on, not a random list that runs on for hundreds of pages.

You can decide where to start, and what needs your time urgently.

What is the critical thing you must do, the one that can't be moved?

It needs to operate fluidly, moving priorities backwards and forwards.

It means you are in control and can dictate to a large extent the direction in which your life is heading.

It also gives you no excuses as you have a plan to regularly review, making you accountable.

Just the conscious act of giving yourself time to think it through and write it down is cathartic.

It is simple but gives you focus, and I hope it will help you.

In my example the children were the most urgent and important, my son was at university completing his final year throughout lockdown and my daughter was taking her GCSEs, so both needed my immediate support, time and attention.

Although the other items on the list were important, they were not urgent. When the exams finished, I could move things around and re-prioritise my focus.

In this example sorting out work and my job came next then finally we could start to plan our wedding.

Question yourself about what is urgent and important, as everything can't be.

What can be moved or changed or removed completely to give you some breathing space and allow you to focus on other priorities?

What are you constantly thinking about that you are never going to do?

If it's not worth a top 3 spot stop thinking about it.

Address it consciously once and for all, and then don't waste the mental energy anymore.

Make some room to think about something more productive or more fun.

Are you making excuses not to move things forward?

Are you holding yourself back fearing changes to your routine and the uncertainty that could follow?

Is the opinion of others making you hesitant?

If you are still listening to that outdated belief system and letting it run your life, don't let it take over your thoughts.

Keep your thinking calm and rational, and don't let anything stop you from being brave and bold with your top 3.

I acknowledge that my example looks quite dull and not hugely aspirational in some ways, in my defence it was lockdown.

Yours might start this way but it will change as you make space in your life and take things off the list.

You will notice how the focus shifts, and you look forward to working through it and then adding your next goal or adventure.

I realise that some things cannot be changed but there are very few that can't be changed in some way. Perhaps passed to someone else, giving you the time to understand which direction you are heading in, towards a better quality of life.

It is your life, you are the driver, use this as the map to point you in the right direction.

I check my top 3 regularly and it does become easier with practice, to think about 3 things.

Moving the subcategories on and off the list as other things take priority, you complete something or find something new and more interesting to spend your time and attention on.

Write your main 3 and sub 3 and set a weekly reminder to check to see where you are at, and what can come off and go on the list.

If you like using colours, code it in a way that works for you, highlight in red the must-do before next week items, and perhaps leisure activities or exciting new challenges might be green.

If you like using numbers prioritise using a numbering system using 1 as urgent and important, each week it will change, some weeks it could be about prioritising an activity or just some time for you.

Whichever way you choose to edit your plan, keep it simple so you continue to use it.

Make sure it is not just a task list, as well as dealing with the things that you must do, include things that are future-facing and that you can look forward to.

In my case planning more leisure time, finding better ways to help us all as a family deal with our stress and wellbeing, and planning and booking a holiday, helped me to deal with the other essential but mundane routines in everyday life.

With a good plan, you finally know where you are heading and what you need to achieve. This allows you to take control and feel less overwhelmed, you have clarity and a vision of what your future will be like, and this gives you more peace of mind.

Now you need to imagine completing the things on your list, moving closer to your goals and dreams, and picturing where you want to be and what you want to do.

When you have completed must-dos on your list, you will have prioritised and created time to add more of what you want to do into your life in the future, so it stops being a remote concept and becomes your weekly life plan.

Focus on all the new things you want to try and how you will not allow your hopes and dreams to be pushed to one side for another week, month, year or even decade.

You have the freedom to choose how you spend your time and you have finally made some time to plan it your way.

What do I want to do?

My career plans were much more exciting when I was 5
Unknown

If you are not yet sure career-wise on which direction to take, whether you are deciding to continue along a well-trodden and established path, or are thinking about trying something new, this simple exercise will help to focus your mind.

Top 3
Your likes and dislikes

What do you like doing?
List the top 3

What do you dislike doing?
List the top 3

What is your school, university, job or homelife asking you to do regularly?
List the top 3 tasks

Question yourself, are these key roles and responsibilities that you are asked to do regularly playing to the things you like, or dislike doing, in the lists above?

What we like doing is usually what we are good at doing, our strengths, some natural and some learned but it suits you and your personality.

What we dislike doing is usually harder, more difficult, and can make us feel uncomfortable.

It is a fine balance to get it right, finding enough challenge without disliking what you do.

It can be hard at first to know which area a new course or job will fall into.

If you only work in areas of your current likes or strengths, you will struggle to grow, but if you are only working doing things you dislike regularly, you are likely to be unhappy in the long term.

A bit of pushing yourself into the dislike zone is good for growth as you try new things or a new way of doing something, but working at something you continue to dislike is awful.

How many of us have sleepwalked into A levels, a university course, or a job, you just keep turning up, without really questioning what you want to do, or why you are doing it, and then you wonder why you are not fulfilled.

It could be that it has been a long-term dream to get onto a specific university course or pursue a particular career, and the reality of your success is not what you thought it would be.

Some wise advice I once received was, "It's okay to change your mind," it really is.

How can you know what something will be like until you try it?

Until you are sitting there learning about it or working in it, it's all just presumption and guesswork.

It is worth taking a long hard look at what you like doing and what you are actually doing, making sure that you are heading in the right direction for your future goals and plans.

Ask yourself does what you are doing now take you nearer to where you ultimately want to be, or are you sitting complaining loudly about your life in the safe zone?

We all have to do things we dislike along the way, just don't make a career out of it.

Finding what you want to do, is a step toward the actions you need to take to make it your reality.

Different personality types

Don't get confused between my personality and my attitude. My personality is who I am, my attitude depends on who you are
Frank Ocean

Knowing your personality type, finding out what makes you tick, and what makes others react to you in the way that they do is useful.

On the internet, there are plenty of free online sites that will evaluate your personality and give you a good insight into yourself.

I have used the companies Myers-Briggs, and Thomas in the past, to assess myself and other colleagues.

They ask a lot of questions, placing you in hypothetical situations to narrow down the type of character that you are.

By gaining an understanding of how you think and feel they can predict how you are likely to act.

If you answer the questions as honestly as possible the findings are insightful.

It is interesting for a group of friends, family members, or work colleagues to read each other's results.

It gives you a better awareness of how everyone thinks and why people react to situations in a certain way.

Finding this out allows you the choice to work out how approaching things differently is more likely to get you the responses you want from other people.

I believe that most people want to be kind, to be a good friend, or to do a good job, however, whatever is going on in their life and yours at that moment, will play a big part in how they react to a decision or situation.

Fundamentally, who they are from their past experiences will also have an impact, we are complicated.

All these factors combine to help or hinder you when making daily decisions, often not rationally as we discovered when we looked at our belief systems.

Your personality is made from your genetics, combined with your upbringing and your personal experiences. You can choose to let this define you forever or you can choose to learn, grow and develop yourself into the person you want to become. Your past experiences can be tricky to move on from, and we all know people who are still stuck in the past unable to move forward after a trauma or tragedy.

Moving forward and leaving people and places behind for whatever reason is hard.

When I left my marriage in 2016, although it was the right decision for everyone, it was heartbreaking, but I survived, and have grown immeasurably since.

The safe and happy family that I had craved all my life and thought I had created, was not my reality. It took a monumental effort to leave, as I was not only physically leaving my marriage behind, but all my childhood dreams and expectations at the same time.

Consequently, my personality type has altered and is different from before.

I have experienced a lot of new things and met a lot of new people which has changed my perception of life, so my future decisions are not the same as decisions I would have made in the past.

Your personality changes as you learn and grow, and many of these personality changing experiences are challenging. Whilst I was overcoming my challenges, more understanding and empathy developed within me.

My children have said that they see sides of my personality that they didn't know existed before, as I allow myself to be vulnerable and to learn to grow and experience new things with childlike wonder and excitement.

The old rules don't apply, as the person I was doesn't exist anymore and with that comes a sense of freedom and a feeling that anything could be possible in my new world.

You have the chance to try on other personalities by challenging yourself to move outside of your comfort zone and try something new.

It could be an activity, a different type of food, travelling to a new city or country, anything you try will broaden your horizons and change your outlook on your own life.

You will absorb those new experiences and they will imprint themselves on who you are, and start to change how you think and feel.

If you use personality testing as a starting point, to understand more about yourself and those around you, as you are learning, growing and changing, you will start to relate better to other people, helping to build stronger, more honest and trusted relationships.

The benefits of having understanding and supportive relationships in your life are huge, both personally and professionally.

Moving forward with others is a joy, and the value of finding people who can understand, stimulate and challenge you in the right way shouldn't be under-estimated.

If you can push yourself to try a few new things regularly, and retest your personality say in 6 months, being honest with your answers, you will find that your personality type has changed somehow.

New experiences help you grow and alter your mindset. The other bonus is that you understand others better, why they behave the way they do is less of a mystery, and they become less infuriating in the process.

Some people have such fixed mindsets nothing is going to move them forward and help them to grow, but very few in my experience, most just need some support and somebody to believe in them.

I have used this type of testing successfully at work with new and existing teams to get a better understanding of each other, team dynamics, and an insight into how best to manage everyone for peak performance.

We have also done this as a family, sometimes the results are surprising, but it is a lot of fun.

Challenge yourself to go out today and speak to someone who you normally avoid speaking to, perhaps a neighbour or a colleague with a very different personality to you.

See if you can find any common ground, try to understand how they see the world, where their views come from, and share something with them about you.

Once you take time to listen to other people, it is easier to relate to them as you understand their thinking and where it might come from.

Your personality, opinions and perspective are allowed to change if you want them to.

Six
No, nine

Management at any level, being one or being managed by one

Management is about persuading people to do things they do not want to do, while leadership is about inspiring people to do things they never thought they could
Steve Jobs

There is no point in recruiting talented people and then micromanaging them to death, leaving everyone involved cross and disappointed when the newest recruit didn't work out.

If you are employing people for their skills, then let them use them to do the job.

I am not saying don't include a comprehensive company induction and training plan, whilst implanting the company vision but if you recruited them to take the pressure off, trust them to make decisions, and catch up regularly to make sure everything is on track.

One person cannot do it all, and if you have identified a need for a role in a business, empowered somebody to do that role, and you trust your judgement, let them get on with it.

If you are the person that is being micromanaged, constantly being checked up on and never given any room to breathe, you have my sympathy.

It is a stifling and very unhealthy way to work.

I imagine you feel, what is the point of suggesting changes when you are not allowed to make any decisions or take any action to prove your knowledge, experience and worth.

This is a time to address how you are being treated and how this makes you feel, and if something doesn't change for you, it's time to move on to be appreciated somewhere else.

But before you walk out the door, question if you can challenge the way you are being managed.

Go in with real examples, and well-planned evidence of how things need to change to make the relationship work better for both parties.

Asking yourself questions like -

What difference will it make to the business if it is done your way?

What will the positive impact be for everyone?

How do things need to change and why?

If you speak knowledgeably and with confidence showing potential solutions to the issues you have come to speak about, the door is more likely to remain open and their ears prepared to listen.

If your arguments are full of blame, negativity and criticism you will be perceived as moaning and complaining, and your manager will switch off after the first few sentences. They will have already decided you are not worth their time or attention.

Planning this type of conversation gives you the advantage, the outcome is not in your hands, but you will know that you gave it your best shot and that is all you can do.

Later in the book, I discuss problem solving and confrontation which might help you in this situation.

The best managers have the same traits as the best parents.

They lead the business and the people that work for them by setting aspirational goals and then persuading their teams they can achieve those goals.

Sometimes they actively join in with their team, at other times they are astute enough to know, that all that is needed is cheerleading from the sidelines.

I find they are patient and instructive in a supportive but not dictatorial way, while nurturing and encouraging you to be the best that you can be, pushing you beyond what you thought was possible.

My middle son played for a football team from the age of 6 to 17, and from years of standing on the edge of the pitch, I know that every parent thinks they are a great manager and believes they could do a better job than the referee.

I also know that just because your voice is the loudest it doesn't make it right.

The same can be said in business, details are important, but if you never see the big picture, the overall goal, and you keep micromanaging everything and everyone, you will stifle growth and lose a lot of good people along the way.

Whether you are the manager or being managed, don't sweat the small stuff springs to mind, a lesson that I finally learned when I had my first child.

I was trying so hard to make him perfect, I initially thought my job as his parent was to continually instruct and relentlessly correct him.

Guess what, the small stuff got bigger as he grew, what started as -

Will the world end if he doesn't eat his peas?

Moved into the teenage years and bigger decisions like what time is reasonable to come home after a party?

The right answer to this depends on if you are the child or the adult and trying to see the other's perspective is hard.

Handing over the right amount of responsibility to my challenging teenager for them to be in control sometimes in their own life, while trying to hang on to some control for my sanity, worked for me.

Another contentious question in our house was -

Is it ok for my new girlfriend to sleep over with me?

The right answer to this one is still unknown as my third child is now asking the same question about her boyfriend.

This is just like being a good manager, getting your life to run the way you want it to, at home and at work, requires the same negotiation skills transferred from one situation to another.

If you can negotiate your way through keeping a room full of 3-year-olds happy and entertained, then managing your boss, and working out how to get the best out of your relationship should be easy, your skills are already there.

Better business

Success is not final; failure is not fatal; it is the courage to continue that counts
Winston Churchill

My top three tips for a successful business are so simple, but rarely are they all followed. Distractions are too easy to justify, resulting in a loss of focus and drive.

I touched on this earlier but think it is worth explaining in more detail.

Firstly, communicate well.

This means both internally, with the people who work with you, and externally, with everyone else that your business has contact with.

The people that you employ or manage should be ambassadors for the business and if you don't have their commitment, and they don't understand your mission, vision and values, whose fault is it?

Well, you have either employed the wrong people (what all of them?) or have failed to translate and competently feed into the business what you stand for and why they should care.

It makes me want to ask the question -

How hard will they work and how committed will they be when you are not around?

It is up to you to inform and direct them well, so they want to do it, not just for you but for themselves.

This is your team, these are your people, you probably spend more time with them than your family, unless they are your family, and that's a whole other difficult dynamic.

So, before you decide that they are all ungrateful and lacking talent, ask yourself some harsh questions at every level of your business.

Has your mission for this business or department been translated and understood by everyone who works for you, and I mean everyone?

Have you explained what it means to you and why it matters?

Are you living the values that you set out to achieve?

Keep these questions at the forefront of your mind, especially at times of change, growth, and uncertainty.

Ask your team and trusted colleagues if they can tell you what you stand for.

It is not enough to presume that people know and understand.

Nearly every business I have ever worked with or for, displayed communication issues.

From multimillion-pound corporations to small start-ups, being clear with communication at all levels is one of the keys to a successful business.

Communicating your message well to the wider world seems obvious, but question yourself about who you want to hear your message, and what they will need to hear to sit up and take notice of you?

I have seen brilliant businesses that have no idea how to talk externally about themselves.

What language they should use to help their message resonate with their audience is a mystery to them.

Often, they are still trying to work out who they need to talk to, and who their message is for, so, they use a broad-brush approach and try to make everything work for everyone, achieving the result that nothing works for anyone.

Make sure that your message represents you as you want it to, and is targeted at the right people, in a way that they can easily understand it.

Secondly, build great relationships with everyone, this means all the people that work with you. If it's a big company and you are at the top this might seem impossible, but it is not.

Are you choosing to pretend it is?

It means regular contact via newsletters, not just spouting corporate messages but letting them get to know who you are and what you stand for.

Always being accessible to them somehow, maybe by e-mail or regular shop floor visits, and never losing touch with what concerns them.

Because the chances are that if it concerns them, it should concern you, and it gives you a chance to head off any storms early.

The people in your business are a valuable and expensive resource, they should share your vision and want to work hard for you.

Work hard to build great relationships with customers, clients, members, the general public, and whoever else you encounter.

Offer the best service, show how you care about these relationships and plan to keep them for the long term.

Loyalty should not be underestimated; people still want to deal with people they like and feel that they can trust.

Be honest if things are not perfect and difficult conversations need to occur. Be as open as you can about a tricky situation, most people are understanding when presented with a genuine apology.

Work hard to build the best relationships you can for the future of the business.

Thirdly, follow a clear, simple and regularly reviewed plan.

If you are not clear in which direction you are heading, you will not know if you are achieving anything. Nobody will want to follow you, as they don't understand what you want from them and how they fit into your plan.

I have worked with a lot of companies who are pleased to have spent a vast amount of time producing massive long-term plans perhaps for the next 10 years. Then they clumsily try to articulate it in the most pompous language possible, throughout the whole business.

I am not saying don't do any longer-term planning, but don't spend immense amounts of time on something that in all probability, will look unrealistic next year.

In the past, short, medium, and long-term planning was regularly given as good advice to follow.

However, the world we live in now is moving so fast, with so many variables that are out of your control you need to make your plan for the near future, with plenty of flexibility and book very regular reviews.

Make sure it translates well at all levels within your business or department and is based on some sort of reality, stretching and aspirational yes, completely impossible no.

It is surprising how complicated we make things, and then we need to spend a lot of precious time and money unravelling them to make them simpler again.

And with change, make sure you are doing it for the right reasons, and identify what needs to change and why.

I have worked with companies who installed change for change's sake and then changed it back again at great expense.

These are great tips for an easier personal life too.

Our personal and professional lives are attached, as I am sure you realise, although I have had many experiences where companies I have worked for think that one shouldn't affect the other.

It is like asking you to switch off a part of yourself as you walk in and out of the building. It is completely unrealistic to think that whatever happens at home won't affect your work life and vice versa.

We are not two people, just one, trying to thrive and survive all that is randomly thrown at us on our journey through our one life.

Revisit your mission, vision and values regularly as one or all of them may need adjusting as you grow and external forces come into play.

This was especially true during Covid when many businesses faced unprecedented trading times. Sadly, a lot of businesses didn't survive, some that could adapt quickly, grew at this challenging time.

You have a responsibility to yourself and others, to be the best that you can be, and in any position of power you could inspire someone else and play a part in their life.

If you can make a positive difference, you have achieved success.

Sometimes the decisions you must make will be difficult, understand why you need to make them, and be as kind and fair with everyone as possible.

First impressions

Each of us is full of too many wheels, screws and valves to permit us to judge one another on a first impression by two or three external signs
Anton Chekhov

You don't ever get a chance to do it again, you must get it right the first time.
No, you don't have to get it right.

We all get it wrong sometimes, and you can usually put it right if you mess up somehow in the beginning.

How many times have you heard?

I didn't like him at first, but he grew on me, and we've now been married for over 30 years.

Some of my best friendships are with people I wasn't sure about at first, they made the wrong initial impression on me as I did on them.

If you are the sort of person who gets very nervous and finds new situations challenging, you might not be at your best. Maybe you have been quickly discounted as a potential new friend when you unintentionally came across as a bit awkward and standoffish.

All the fantastic qualities that you have may need a bit more reassurance before you are prepared to let them surface, so perhaps in an interview situation the first impression that you give might not be great.

It's so important to give each other a bit of time and start to dig deeper, not just rely on that first impression.

I do believe that the quietest people have the loudest minds, I am not one of those quiet people.

Maybe you are one of those people who overcompensate and try to be everyone's friend immediately, desperately showing off and trying to impress with outlandish story after outlandish story to prove your worth.

However, underneath it all is the need for acceptance, to fit in and be allowed to join the gang, sometimes the first version is not who you are at all.

Some people present brilliantly at interviews, that's the bit they are great at, with a well-crafted and practised presentation. But, when they start the job, you wonder where the interview version of them has gone, your first impression was incorrect.

I know it is hard not to judge what a person is like based on their first impression, it's human nature to assess quickly with our fight or flight response. You want to know, are they a friend or a threat, but few of us are our actual selves when we are put under pressure in this way.

I'm not suggesting that you must like everyone, but I do completely dispute the idea that you only get one chance to get it right.

Judging anything solely on a first impression means you miss out on so much, not just people, trying new things more than once is necessary.

What's unfamiliar usually feels uncomfortable and difficult at first as it takes a few goes to relax, if you only try it once you will never give yourself that chance.

A lot of initially challenging customers have become my biggest advocates. When I got it wrong with them at first or misjudged a business deal in some way, I admitted my mistake, took ownership of the situation, apologised, and changed the outcome for the long term.

We have a culture where someone must be to blame for everything that happens in life, but sometimes things just happen, you get it wrong, and you can be sorry without needing someone to blame.

Admitting you got it wrong at first, is not easy, some of us find it easier than others.

It can be seen as some sort of weakness or failure when in reality, it is the opposite, you need strength, courage and confidence to admit to something.

Self-awareness is important, if you know what type of first impression you make on other people, you can explain that you get nervous, and practice techniques to relax more.

If you are prone to talking a lot because you suffer with nerves, you can learn to stop talking as much and actively listen, being more present and relevant with what you say.

If you get it wrong with someone, have humility and understanding, ask to move on from the situation, and if someone gets it wrong with you, try to have empathy, listen and move on, and genuinely let it go.

I know people who hold onto these stories, showcasing the perceived failure of others, bringing them out like trophies as they update everyone on how disappointing it is.

Life is too short to collect examples of when you or they got things wrong.

Move on, forgive yourself and others, and try to do better next time.

Presenting

They may forget what you said, but they will never forget how you made them feel
Carl W. Buechner

Present with passion and enthusiasm, if you are not excited about what you are saying why should anyone else be?

This applies when presenting yourself, presenting anything to an audience, appearing with others online and in every situation in life where you are turning up.

Life is one long presentation in one form or another.

I understand presenting comes more naturally to some people than others, you don't have to be loud to be engaging, often the opposite is true.

Having enthusiasm about what you are talking about is infectious for whoever your audience may be.

It might be an interview you are attending or presenting to hundreds of people when you speak on a big stage. These people have agreed to give you their time, so use it well and put the time in, to practice and prepare properly.

What you present should be bespoke in some way, tailored for them, and make sure that the material you use can be easily understood, always think of your audience first.

Put yourself in their shoes before you start to plan anything.

Part of my work is helping people to present, to develop their confidence and their individual style. Getting any message across to an audience is a skill and writing a powerful presentation that lands with impact takes time and practice.

If you are presenting yourself for a further education course or a potential job, practice with friends and family, asking and answering the type of questions you might be asked.

Answering questions in this way then begins to feel natural and you can get your key points in your mind before you do it for real.

This will make you feel more confident and prepared, as your brain relaxes when you are asked familiar questions, it already knows how to answer so it doesn't go into panic mode.

Nerves are natural and show you care and most of us get them.

Good preparation will help, and remember that you are likely to be the subject expert when you are speaking, no one knows if you miss a bit or pause for a little too long.

The same rules apply when presenting to an audience from the stage.

It is just like going to the theatre where all the actors have rehearsed their parts, you are the actor in this scenario so you should know your part well.

I am not saying act it out and stop being you, being able to be comfortable and coming across as authentic is half the battle.

Know the order of your presentation and like it.

Make sure you practice in front of a lot of other people, take their feedback on board, and see how you look in front of the mirror.

Is the way you stand giving off the right message, do you look confident?

Work out the key messages that you want to tell them and help them to understand why they should want to listen to you.

Most of us can only remember 3 to 5 messages so don't overload them with too much information, their brains will object and switch off.

You need to be sure about why you are presenting this information.

If you care about your subject this will show, as your well-thought-out plan takes them on a journey they don't want to miss.

It doesn't have to be slides, it can be an e-mail or a focused conversation, presentations come in many different forms as we communicate our messages.

I have delivered some great presentations and had fantastic feedback, I have also had some epic failures in the beginning.

I once presented to a large audience in Newcastle, my presentation was all about changing your life and included talking about how short life is and the death of my parents.

It was a tried and tested presentation that I changed slightly depending on the audience after I had conducted some research about them.

It was not as depressing as I have just made it sound.

What I hadn't banked on was that my audience of 250 people from the leisure industry would be having far too much fun at their annual company event.

This had something to do with the fact that they had all been in the free bar for the whole afternoon and early evening.

My original slot was moved while I was there, from 6.30pm to 9.30pm and I was too inexperienced to realise that I was heading for a car crash.

Only a comedian with the ability to answer a barrage of hecklers would do, and my half-hour slot felt like a week.

I tried and failed to be brilliant.

Afterwards, I understood that although I had been booked by the management with the best of intentions, as their ambition was to make their staff think about their lives and inspire them, the staff's ambition however started and ended at the free bar.

It was a case of the wrong presentation and presenter for that audience, and we all left feeling unhappy.

I learnt that night that I am not a comedian, and never to present to an audience when alcohol is the main event.

You can only try your best, but simple techniques can help to craft your presentation, focusing firmly on your audience, ditching death by PowerPoint forever, to leave you feeling that you have achieved something great.

PART 4

How am I feeling right now?

Remembering the good times

Health

Grief and dealing with death

Professional help

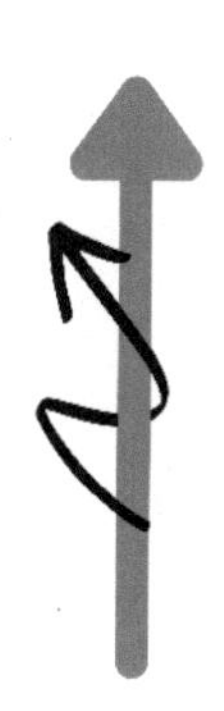

How am I feeling right now?

I hide all my scars with an I'm fine
Unknown

Imagine that you are standing up and next to the top of your head is the number 10, you are feeling fantastic mentally and physically.

It is one of those bright and shiny days that we all want more of.

The following day is not a great day, looking down at your feet there is a number 1, nothing against your feet, but they are at the bottom of your body, so it works in this illustration to identify how you feel.

It is my scale of wellness; I use it to work out how I am feeling several times a day.

My tummy (my husband says I am too old to use this word, but I like it) often features, as this is number 5 for me, it is not a scientific scale!

Recognising where you are mentally and emotionally, quickly and easily, means that you can do things to change how you are feeling if you need to.

Boosting your mood could be as simple as needing to eat something, resting, taking some exercise, talking to a friend, deep breathing, reading, watching a film or just taking 10 minutes out.

Something to get you back to a higher number having enhanced your mood, rather than allowing yourself to fall further down towards your feet.

When you identify how you feel, and are aware of what makes you feel this way it allows you to break cycles and regular patterns of behaviour to achieve alternative outcomes.

It's easy to become so used to feeling a certain way that it becomes an addiction as any other state of feeling is unfamiliar and uncomfortable.

When reverting to a route of familiar sadness or disappointment feels like the only way to live, it's time to act.

My scale of wellness, although simplistic, does work for me, it stops me from returning down some familiar, destructive and self-critical pathways.

It makes me think about how I can quickly put in some corrective action, as I won't let myself sit in the low numbers for long, I actively do something to alter my mood.

It is useful to have a measure that is consistent for you, so you can regularly check in with yourself and become self-aware enough to act if a lot of low numbers start appearing more frequently.

If you are stuck and struggling to move up the scale, outside help would be the right answer.

If this scale doesn't work for you find your own system.

This works for me because how I feel physically in my body, hugely affects how I feel mentally and the stress levels in my mind.

Getting up and going outside always helps me to move my number up.

Give yourself small things to look forward to throughout the day, it makes each day a lot more enjoyable, who doesn't want some high points every day? Whatever you can do to treat yourself without having to spend any money or take up a lot of time usually works.

This scale is not about making those massive life changes, it is about forming daily positive habits that help you to move through each day with a bit more sunshine.

My Scale of Wellness

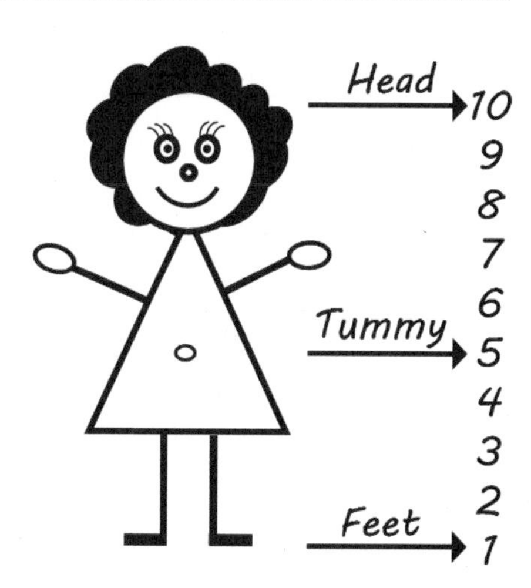

Remembering the good times for when things aren't so great

Don't cry because it's over. Smile because it happened
Dr Seuss

Lots of people recommend journalling every day the things that you are grateful for, so you can look back and reflect when you need motivation or a reminder to appreciate your life.

As we have discussed, when going through difficult times, writing can help to make things clearer, to look back and see how far you have come from challenging times and places.

The simple act of writing things down helps to rest your busy head, getting it all out, both positive and negative is powerful.

It will help you to realise that things aren't always as bad as you think, and you do have lots of good times that will happen again.

Having it written down is a reminder for you and acts as evidence to persuade your brain of this. It is a real fact, it was your reality, you wrote it down.

If you can get into the daily writing habit and it helps you, then do it.

However, for me, it can feel like another item on the to-do list.

If I put a must-do daily label on it and struggle to find anything to say, it becomes something I have failed to achieve, when I don't manage it every day it causes me more stress.

Instead, I record things that happen that make me smile, special meals out, people I have spent time with, holidays, and things that make me happy, with just a few notes in a diary.

Another way that works for some people is to write down on a slip of paper, something good about your day or week that you are happy about or grateful for, it can be anything, it is yours.

Post them in a jar for a year and take them out at the end of the year or indeed anytime you like to help you remember all the great things that happened. Useful to keep, open, and read through if you need some motivation.

Start now by listing 3 events that you want to remember, they can be anything and write in as much detail as you want.

I find that if I mention the weather, what I ate, any music that was playing at the time, basically what excited my senses, I can remember things in a lot more detail.

Recording not just the bare facts but how it felt to be there will trigger more memories.

These techniques may sound very simple, but they can be incredibly powerful ways to improve the way you feel, so they're well worth a try.

Health

It is health that is real wealth not pieces of gold and silver
Mahatma Gandhi

Firstly, I am not qualified in any way to give diet or exercise advice, I can only speak from my experience of trying to be thin.

We all know that almost everyone who eats too many calories will put on weight, some people are happy to be larger and that's fine.

I am more concerned about being strong and healthy, so I am not limited physically from what I want to do.

When I was heavier, doing daily tasks felt harder and I had less energy, so I joined a gym, something I have done a few times at different points in my life. It didn't work too well for me as I hadn't planned it properly, I gave it no importance in my weekly plan, and I hadn't put it on my top 3 as a priority.

A few years after my last gym attempt, I started running with a friend.

This was not until I was in my mid-40s, and over the first few months we started slowly, we had no choice as I couldn't make it to the end of the street without needing to walk.

It was starting to exercise with a friend that motivated me to continue, and as we started to improve, we could chat, if we weren't going uphill.

At the end of a run, I felt like I had offloaded some daily stress whilst enjoying listening to the latest news from my friend's life.

We were attending an unofficial counselling session and so I was motivated to keep running for two reasons.

Firstly, I didn't want to let my friend down, so I showed up, I had committed to her.

Secondly, I knew we were making progress, we were losing weight, and we both started to feel healthier and had more energy.

This didn't happen overnight it took a few months, but we persisted together.

It made me question my health choices in other areas of my life. Looking at what I was eating and drinking, I started to make better choices.

Even though our running was still slow, the buzz we felt afterwards and the sense of achievement when we got a bit further and faster, kept us coming back for more.

I did later push this competitive need to do better too far when I moved out of the area and started running alone.

I became mildly obsessed with distances and times, needing to control and critique my performance, constantly measuring improvement, sucking any joy out of just running.

As I mentioned earlier in the book, I had to ditch the watch, as I almost destroyed my enjoyment of simply running because I can.

We don't all want to run, but I know if you can find something to make you physically fitter it is easier to mentally cope with the personal and professional challenges in your life.

I am not a health fanatic, I do what I enjoy, and doing it regularly is the key. Once you realise you don't need to be good at it, if you are having a good time, know that it's beneficial.

I try to eat healthily about 80% of the time, using the 80/20 rule.

If you are unfamiliar with this rule, it simply means that I eat well 80% of the time, and treat myself 20% of the time. I don't go mad, but I enjoy some treats sometimes.

I could be more disciplined, but I want to enjoy my life, and this balance of exercise and eating well works for me.

Nourishing your mind and body like putting fuel in your car, gives you the best chance of peak performance.

Lack of quality sleep, poor food choices, and no exercise do not result in you being the best that you can be, it results in the tired and grumpy version rising to the surface.

Choosing an activity with others not only brings health benefits but often a new friendship group.

Taking the first step is the hardest, quashing your inner voice as it tries to persuade you that it's not for you, you can't do it.

Try switching that voice to a more rational one.

"If all these other people can do it then so can I, and I know if I try and fail, I can try something else."

I would argue that you can never fail if you have tried, you are trying out things to see what fits you.

It is the testing stage, the fact-finding part, you know in advance that you will not like everything, but chances are you will like something.

It is finding out what will work for you, and what you can sustain as your lifestyle over the long term.

It is relatively easy to stick to the latest fad diet or revolutionary new exercise class for a few weeks. The challenge comes when you need to return to your normal life again, go out for dinner, drink alcohol, attend a friend's birthday party or turn up for a work event.

Trying to stick to extremely strict rules, unless for medical reasons is unachievable for most of us and we berate ourselves for not achieving the unattainable goals we have set.

This results in giving up anything health or exercise related altogether and deciding it's not for us.

It is ok to be the tortoise in the race of life and let the hare shoot past with its latest crazy ideas for diets and exercise in many guises.

We know who wins in the end!

I am slowly and steadily winning the exercise race and you can too, by including it in your weekly plan until it becomes a habit you don't want to break.

By realistically setting your health goals you will succeed.

Look at the time you have available, and other commitments in your life and make it fit.

If you miss a walk, run, swim or gym session, don't beat yourself up about it, pick it up again the next day.

The same goes for following any healthy eating plan, if you have a difficult day get back on track tomorrow.

Don't dwell on it or persuade yourself that you knew you would fail so what's the point.

Developing your mindset to accept that you deserve the best of health and making a move to achieve this is the best gift you can give yourself.

Grief and dealing with death

It can swallow you whole, then release you sporadically to gulp more air and stop you from drowning for a while, before it pulls you under again
Sally Measom

For me it did feel like I was slowly drowning, surfacing long enough to be surprised by the fact that the world was remarkably unchanged around me.

I had no understanding of why my loss hadn't changed everyone else when such a seismic shift had happened to me.

On the surface, I continued normally in my daily life as a wife and mother. But underneath, I was being plunged into more despair and confusion every time I remembered how my world had been changed forever by the loss of my mum.

Being an only child is a lonely place to be when you lose your one remaining parent.

The effect of the death of someone close on your mental health, and the strength you need to find just to keep going, to get you out of bed or into it in the first place, is exhausting.

When faced with devastation, processing your new reality requires a mammoth effort.

Dealing with the death of a loved one puts every other part of your life into perspective, and you wonder why you spent so much time worrying about trivial things in the past.

The unsettling realisation that nothing will ever be the same again, rolled over and over in my mind as I struggled to imagine my future.

Even though my mum's death was expected and a welcome release from pain, I still found the finality of it shocking.

I felt for a long time like a tangible hole had appeared where a piece of me was missing.

From starting to process the emotional waves of despair, to the vast number of decisions you need to make at the most vulnerable time of your life is exhausting.

I still ruminate over the fact that after my mum was cremated, I agreed to her ashes being scattered in the summer garden, when I am sure she would have preferred to finally rest in spring.

We can't always get it right, and those that have died would forgive us I am sure, as we try to navigate our way through this necessary but overwhelming process.

I don't believe that you ever get over the loss of such a treasured person, but I know that you can learn to live with it.

When I could think about more than just the end of her life, I knew I was moving into another phase of grief.

The signs of a future that I felt I could be present in, coincided with positive memories of my mum starting to emerge.

Being told that time heals is not useful to anyone, when each day stretches out in front of you looking like some sort of vast wasteland, it is not a comforting thought.

At times, in the beginning of my grief, it felt like my tangible hole was causing physical hurt drilling deep inside me with varying degrees of pressure and pain. Those seconds in the morning before you remember the enormity of what has happened, act as a cruel reminder of your previous life, before being jolted painfully back to your new reality.

I talked about my loss to trusted friends, and although they couldn't understand my pain, being able to verbalise my feelings more and more helped me with the process.

Acceptance must take centre stage for you to be able to move forward.

If you feel like you are struggling, think about getting some help, then act on that thought, the earlier in the process the better.

Inside me now, the hole is replaced with a box full of memories as I have processed what happened.

I can talk about my mum and remember all the good and infuriating parts of our relationship.

This doesn't mean I am not sad sometimes, but I have a duty to my mum, husband, and children to live my life well.

I now feel that those who have died are safe and settled, in a comfortable place, forever a part of me.

Remembering all parts of my mum and not giving her a saintlier status in death than in life, helps me to keep a realistic picture of my memories.

Parts of my childhood are suddenly triggered at random times by a certain smell or a phrase someone uses that is very familiar. These moments are now comforting and make me smile, keeping the memory of my mum alive.

Don't leave it too late to speak to those in your life that you love about their life.

There are hundreds of questions I wish I had asked my mum, particularly about her childhood and teenage years.

Take the time to ask and learn about the life they had before you were a part of it, one day it will be too late.

Experiencing death changes us all, if you can't move on, it can define who you are for the rest of your life.

Death is a part of life, and you can use it as a motivator to change your life.

When grieving we all go through a similar process, although the specifics of our experiences are unique it is often helpful to know you are not alone, and that what you are going through is normal.

As a child, aged 7, I lost my dad, if I could have shared my grief with other children in the same situation, I am sure it would have helped immensely. But it was the 80s, and we didn't talk about it, the thinking was that it was better to ignore it and move on.

Nobody mentioned how to achieve moving on, as we didn't talk about it!

At school aged about 8, we were asked to write one thing we wanted to happen in our life, answers included becoming an astronaut, a dancer, or a pilot.

My answer was that I wanted my daddy to come back.

This was put up on the wall alongside all the other answers and viewed by many teachers and other parents and still, no one spoke to me about the death of my dad.

I have kept this piece of paper for all these years.

That little girl is always there inside me, but now I understand her better, I can reassure her, and we can move on.

I am pleased and relieved that the thinking has changed through the decades, and talking is now recommended as we learn to process the changes in our lives.

I am not sure how avoiding things and not allowing your thoughts and feelings to surface to have their voice, is ever helpful.

It took me until my late 40s to start properly dealing with my childhood grief, I am the proof that it is never too late to ask for help.

My husband helped me to work out why I behave the way I do, to look inside and take out the tightly packed boxes that I had locked away in an attempt to protect myself.

To re-examine my experience with death and to work through the hurt that had become so fundamental to who I was.

It was limiting me from myself, I was unable to be vulnerable as it felt like weakness, having had to be strong for so many years, through such a huge trauma in my childhood.

My husband is well versed in this subject.

He lost his older brother when his brother was 17 and he was only 12, and his sister died when she was in her 40s. He struggled for a long time with the guilt of surviving when two of his siblings had died.

We were and are therapy for each other, and subconsciously we had a connection and deep empathy for how the other one felt.

A fundamental understanding of why we behave and react to things in a certain way, that's not to say we feel the same about everything, but similar experiences are a connecting factor.

It gives us both the perspective that life is too short to waste.

It is never too late, you can address the things that you have hidden away as too difficult or too painful, by opening yourself up and dealing with the damage.

I am not suggesting that this is easy, or you launch headlong into this alone. Speak to family and friends, find a doctor or counsellor to help you to find a way through, and perhaps a self-help group, with people who will understand and can empathise with your pain.

Lots of books have been written on the subject, find one that can help you to process what you are going through, this might be a good place to start.

Not having to carry the burden of those boxes around inside anymore gives you space to pack new happier ones in their place. The sense of lightness and relief you will feel make it worth dealing with.

Professional help

Depression lies, it tells you you've always felt this way, and you always will. But you haven't, and you won't
Halley Cornell

If life is proving too much, where getting through each day feels impossible, or your thoughts are very dark, go to your doctor, speak to a trusted friend or family member and get some help.

There is absolutely no shame in reaching out and asking for help.

Sometimes you just need to talk to someone with another perspective, it's as if your brain is stuck and can't move forward on its own.

Sometimes it is a lot more serious and longer-term help might be needed.

Realising that you need help with how you are thinking, feeling or behaving is the first step towards achieving an alternative outcome for your life.

You can trick yourself with negative thoughts on repeat, unable to find a way out of this dark pattern with no path in sight.

Every task can seem like a huge challenge, as you lack the motivation needed to actively participate in your own life.

Past failings become amplified as positive experiences and memories fade into the background.

You feel helpless, a failure, worthless, you don't see the point in anything as you spiral into a thought pattern that is the new narrative of who you have become.

At this point, you might be starting to isolate yourself from other people, as you shut yourself off from the rest of the world.

Deciding for them, that they shouldn't spend their time with you, as you know you are not worth the effort.

If this is how you feel, you need to get help.

I had a particularly low point that took me completely by surprise in my early 50s, having never suffered anything like it before.

It was debilitating at the time, and after I successfully received professional help, it left me with a much greater understanding of how other people feel. How anxious they regularly are, and how negatively depression affects their day-to-day life, sometimes for years.

It also reminded me that we are all going through our struggles, and the impact on each of us is unique.

In my case the catalyst was exhaustion from too much work in a very stressful environment, the triggers are different for us all and what you can deal with is not the same as anyone else.

No one is immune from mental health problems, no matter how successful or confident you may be.

We are all on our bumpy path full of peaks and troughs, and we need to find a way that works for us.

In my case, the warning signs were there as I got less patient, more tearful, angrier, and much more distracted, unable to commit to or concentrate on anything other than work.

I chose to ignore the signs, even when physical symptoms tried to make me sit up and listen. I was regularly dizzy, faint, and had a sick feeling almost all of the time.

Although at this low point in my life, I didn't spiral into alcohol or drug abuse, I can understand why people make very poor choices to self-medicate in a misguided effort to lift their mood for a short time, trying to find some release.

Looking at what triggered the feelings in the first place, for me, it was diagnosed as stress-related, developing some robust coping mechanisms and strategies, alongside counselling, and possibly medication, will help you find a way through.

It is important to recognise how and why it started, so you know when you are heading in the same direction again. This gives you the chance to catch it early, alter its course and get you back on track.

Having been in control of a lot of things for a long time, I was left feeling helpless, very sad, and like I had lost who I was as a person.

The fundamental characteristics of what made me, me, had disappeared.

This new and baffling experience where I couldn't find myself was scary.

But with support, time, and being kind to myself, this gave me a chance to question what I wanted out of my life.

As I started to recover, I reviewed the way I thought about a number of things and started valuing what was important to me, work easily dropped off the top of the list.

My top priorities now included the people in my life and my time. I had to re-evaluate what I wanted to do, who I wanted to do it with and how much time I wanted to spend doing it.

I changed direction and have become much happier finding a good balance, being healthy in both my mind and body and feeling fulfilled in my home and work life.

Taking some stress out of my life was a choice I had to make to positively thrive not just to survive.

It is a good positive step for you to ask for and accept help, so if you need it, ask for it.

You deserve to feel as well as you can, and whoever that involves on your journey to get there, go and find them now.

PART 5

Where do you spend your time?

Social media

Money

Travel with no expectations

Where do you spend your time?

Where you are going to spend your time and your energy is one of the most important decisions you get to make.
Jeff Bezos

Draw a chart with days of the week on the left-hand side, and across the top write your own headings for what you spend your time on throughout the week, like the example below.

Day	Sleep	Exercise	Work	TV	Social media	Social life	Totals	Missing hours
Mon	8	—	9	2	2	—	21	3
Tue	8	1	9	3	—	2	23	1
Wed	8		9	4	2		23	1
Thu	8	1	9	2	4	—	24	0
Fri	6	—	9	—	3	6	24	0
Sat	10	1.5	—	6	2.5	4	24	0
Sun	9	2	—	4	1	8	24	0
Weekly total	57	5.5	45	21	14.5	20	163	5

Missing hours need to be accounted for, you have either not put in the correct number of hours somewhere or not put in all the necessary headings.

If you put the amount of time, you spend doing each task in the boxes over a typical week, you will work out what is zapping your time. This can be an eye-opening surprise, but it will allow you to focus and address the balance if necessary.

It can be as detailed as you like, hour by hour or am and pm only, it depends on how many activities you do in a day. If it is easier to use a separate sheet of paper for each day, then do so.

Some tasks must be done, such as looking after your children if you have them, often other tasks are avoidable.

You might find you are spending time on them out of old habits, or a misplaced sense of loyalty without actively realising just how much of your life they are taking up.

In a work environment, I use this time management exercise for team members to record what they are doing with their time at work.

I usually find that some weekly tasks can be changed, dropped completely, or delegated, freeing up more time to spend on the important things that the business wants to prioritise.

It is just the same in your home and personal life, unless you review what you are doing with your time, you don't seem to have enough of it, and then it disappears forever.

With minor adjustments and a bit of planning, you will find more time to do the things you enjoy doing, on your quest to design the life that you want to live.

Social media

In case of FIRE please leave the building before posting it on social media!
Unknown

Is social media the way to present the best version of you?

No, it usually involves presenting a false version as everyone competes for who has the most perfect life.

You can't win and there is no end, trying and feeling like you are always failing in the unattainable quest for perfection causes anxiety, stress and depression.

A feeling of not being good enough, breeds a sense of worthlessness, spending time trying to achieve the unachievable is madness.

As a society, we are in danger of producing a range of clones, when individuality and celebrating your differences are out of fashion and you need to look like a celebrity to be accepted.

In my experience, this is particularly prevalent with the younger generation as they struggle to accept themselves, continually being bombarded by images of perceived perfection is not helpful.

When you scratch the surface, you find that we are all flawed, going through the same feelings and emotions, and celebrities are the same, but it often comes with more pressure.

Then if they spectacularly fall from grace, they get knocked down and social media enjoys informing you that they are not as perfect as they should be. Guess what, they are only human and are allowed to make mistakes too.

Destroying people in this way, I find appalling.

If everything you ever got wrong in your life, the things you deeply regret or caused you embarrassment were suddenly made public all over social media how would you feel?

Random strangers who have no knowledge of who you are or what you have been through, feel entitled to have an opinion about you and are excited by how you have failed.

They delight in your flaws and are desperate to share them with the widest possible audience.

What sort of life do you have if destroying others in this way is what makes your life seem better?

To find the true value in people, you must look below their shiny surface, beyond their exterior pictures, and ask yourself -

What do they stand for?

Who are they really?

Do I like what they believe in and how they treat others in their life?

Rarely do any of us show the worst of ourselves to the outside world, you present your best face on social media as you do at work.

It is usually at home, in private, with those you trust when you can be yourself.

If you dream and aspire to be like someone on social media, be careful that what and who you aspire to be like are worth it and exist as you imagine in the first place.

An obsession with social media means that even at home you present an outside face, not able to relax unless you can show the world how you are relaxing. Constantly photographing, recording and sharing, desperate for the approval of others. You are unable to appreciate what is around you, in fact, you don't really know, as being present in the moment and absorbing an experience with all your senses doesn't happen anymore.

Living your life constantly on social media is dangerous.

Studies have shown that social media is addictive, when you get a like on your post, you get a dopamine high, just like an addict gets from cocaine.

If you are one of those people who can't get out of bed without checking your Facebook, this is the same behaviour as an alcoholic who can't get out of bed without a drink.

Perhaps you can't get into bed unless your phone is beside you at night, doesn't this sound a little bit mad?

I am suggesting that you take an honest look at your relationship with social media and choose carefully what you look at.

Absorbing more perfection can only result in feelings of inadequacy, and a feeling that you don't measure up.

Think about what you are regularly letting seep into your mind.

This applies to other media as well, if you are bombarding yourself with bad news it is exhausting.

You will begin to feel that life is hopeless and out of your control.

This combined with not feeling good enough when everyone else appears more beautiful, successful, confident, and popular than you, is the recipe for making yourself feel terrible, and can send you into a downward spiral that is hard to stop.

As I write this, the latest statistics show that we spend an average of two hours and twenty four minutes a day on social media.

Does that surprise you, or horrify you, maybe you spend a lot more time on it than this?

What would happen if you switched it all off sometimes?

Don't let it dominate your life, wean yourself off your regular behaviour pattern, change your habit and limit your exposure.

Switch off and see how it feels, talk down the panic if it sets in, you are unlikely to be missing anything important, then enjoy the freedom that it brings.

Reduce the time, attention, and importance you give social media in your life, and get out and meet real people. Reconnect with friends and family, and prioritise your health and happiness, not just the quick fix of something that in the long term is meaningless for you.

Choose to move on from focusing on other people's lives, start to spend time on your life, and discover things that will help you to learn and grow.

Real people who might appear to be living ordinary lives are often extraordinary, it's up to you to go out and find them.

I realise that not all social media is damaging, it's how I met my husband so it can't be all bad, but more of that later.

From the millions of social media sites, seek out the good stuff and connect with the interesting people, the ones you feel a connection with.

Find the groups that interest you and those who care about more than just how they look.

Don't let social media steal all your time, it provides endless rabbit holes to fall into, leaving you wondering how you got to where you are and questioning what you are looking at and why.

Be in charge of your actions, you control what you view.

Think about how it influences you and alters your mindset, often in a negative way.

You need to find a balance, a life outside your computer and phone.

If you spent less time on social media you would have more time to spend on an activity that improves your life, how would this make you feel?

Money

Nowadays people know the price of everything and the value of nothing
Oscar Wilde

I am rich by some people's measurement of wealth and thought of as poor by others, depending upon where you are in the world, your upbringing, how much money you have personally, and how you view and value money.

I thought a lot about writing this section, as my relationship with money has not always been that great.

At times in my life, I have had more than my close friends and not always used it wisely, saved very little, spent a lot, sometimes without a great deal of thought. At other times in my life, I have had a lot less.

I do know that money cannot buy you happiness.

Some of the people I used to know that are the richest are the most unhappy. Somehow, as you buy more things, spending more on bigger and better, gives you more to worry about.

Having said that, it is a very trivial point, when the depressing fact of not having enough money to heat your house and feed your family is becoming an increasing reality for many people.

It is easy to be flippant and talk about money in a way that excludes a lot of people when you have some and others have very little.

I am clearly not an expert, but when I had enough money to cover the basics and I had some leftover, I wish I had spent less and saved some for unexpected events, it seems like a sensible choice to me now.

You need to decide what you want to spend your money on, and how much money you consider enough, is very different from anyone else.

I have worked with multi-million-pound corporations, small charities, and social enterprises and the comparison between the have and have-nots is vast. I have regularly found that those who have very little, are more willing to share what they have, perhaps just a simple meal, frequently looking out for friends and neighbours.

Often, they are living in a close community, whilst those who are more affluent are not aware of who their neighbours are, so I wonder who is the richest?

I remember one of the happiest families I ever met lived in a tiny 2 bedroomed terrace house with 6 people happily living alongside one another.

I am not making a judgement that one life is better than another, sometimes, however, I am astounded by the kindness of relative strangers who are willing to share what little they have.

The amount that different occupations get paid is puzzling.

It feels unbalanced to materially reward social media, TV, and football stars in such an out-of-proportion way.

When compared to what we pay the people who look after others, the ones who care for the most vulnerable, those who cannot care for themselves due to sickness and disability, and young children that have had a challenging start.

Where we place our reward and value as society looks proportionally very misplaced.

One of the richest men in the world, Steve Jobs, who was Apples CEO, apparently said-

"Your true inner happiness does not come from the material things of this world. Whether you are flying first-class or economy class if the plane crashes, you crash with it."

As his life deteriorated, he is said to have reflected on his life and talked about no one else being able to carry his disease for him.

If choosing between health and wealth, I think you would choose health every time.

I have learnt that money is not the most important thing for me to strive for and achieve in life. It was once my main goal, and it can be a lonely and hollow victory when this is what motivates you to move forward.

It is no longer what drives me or makes me feel that I have done a great job. It is important that I have enough to be comfortable and again that's a unique perspective for us all, having more in the past made me no happier, and I have chosen to place my values elsewhere.

I am lucky, I have enough to be able to make choices about what I do with my life, and have free time to choose, maybe this is the key to me having enough.

This did come as a result of deciding to live in a smaller house, have cheaper holidays, and spend less on just about everything.

It is a small price to pay for my time and the freedom to choose what I do with the rest of my life.

When you go shopping and buy things, it gives you a short-term high, your body releases dopamine and serotonin. It gives you a sensation of instant gratification making you feel happy, that's why it feels so good but not for long.

Then you come crashing down and need to buy more things that you don't need, to get the same feeling, and for your body to release the drug again.

Don't get sucked into this dangerous repetitive cycle, there are other healthier ways to get this sort of high.

Learn to enjoy what you have, someone else will always have more or less than you.

Most importantly, value the people in your life, the way your friends and family love you unconditionally, they should cherish you, money or no money.

If you want to get a picture of where your money goes, and I highly recommend you do this if you don't already, you can start with your bank.

Lots of banks have great apps to help you track your spending, if that doesn't work for you, write it down or record it on your phone.

Write down the main headings for what you spend your money on, for example -

Essentials - Nice to have - Savings -

Then list everything you spend under one of these headings and add it up daily or weekly.

Being very honest about what is essential, mortgage, rent, heat, light and everyday food come into this category, however, takeaways do not!

Nice to have for me would include items like holidays, theatre trips and meals out.

Look at what you can change, move or stop doing, to balance your money better.

The essentials have to be covered first, writing down everything you spend your money on will start to put you in control.

Then you can set yourself a simple weekly budget under each of the headings.

You will more than likely know the amount of money coming in, and now have a good idea of what will be going out, by bringing it all under your control you are in charge of it.

Your money shouldn't control you, and to be surprised about where your money has gone is never a good thing.

Putting your head in the sand is not an option, the time and energy you spend worrying, and the fear about what might or might not happen is overwhelming when you have money problems.

Take control of your money, develop better spending habits, and then you can move on with your life.

If you are having serious money problems do not despair, there are people who can help you, and a quick internet search will provide a place to start.

Your bank is also worth talking to and should point you in the right direction.

Talking to someone is the first step to sorting it out once and for all, no matter how much money you do or don't have.

Travel with no expectations

To travel is to take a journey into yourself
Danny Kaye

I am still learning to travel with no expectations and need to remind myself regularly that it is supposed to be an adventure that I have chosen to take. I also need to remember that it is ok to leave some things to chance, meticulous planning of every second before going anywhere, is not required.

When I finally book my holiday, choosing it is a process not to be rushed.

I pinball from some hot deserted island to looking at the northern lights with one quick click of my mouse, considering all possibilities and then end up happily in the UK.

I find that when travelling, it is not as simple as time away from home feeling any better or worse than my everyday life, judging it this way is problematic. It is different and unfamiliar, so it is an unfair measure to use, as undoubtedly it takes a short time for me to adjust to my new surroundings.

I live it in my head repeatedly before I arrive, I have already imagined everything about it and have made my presumptions.

I have built up so many expectations that I am bound to be unhappy with something as it is not what I thought it would be.

If I am not careful, I close myself off from experiencing the reality of where I am and the exciting unpredict-ability of being on holiday or somewhere else for a while, where spontaneous decisions allow me to discover something new. This usually ends up being the most enjoyable part of the trip as it was so unexpected.

I have been surprised in far-flung destinations by random experiences, including feeding a camel in Tunisia with a plant directly from my mouth to theirs.

I do question why I chose to do this, and why I partake in other mad adventures but I have never regretted trying new things, it's usually great fun.

I include in this, jumping from what I considered to be a very tall ledge in Croatia, into a running river below.

My husband and children would argue that their ledge was much higher than mine, but it was a great achievement for me, although I do not feel I will ever need to repeat it.

I have also had random experiences closer to home.

As I was showing off how I could stand up in a canoe, the inevitable happened, I tipped into the water quite spectacularly.

I even sat outside a nearby café with my family afterwards, dripping wet, proclaiming I was fine, my pride was still intact.

I would love to say that this was years ago, but sadly I cannot, I was over 50 at the time.

I am still learning to pack an open mind along with my suitcase when I travel anywhere, and I try hard to leave all my expectations at home.

Travelling doesn't have to mean that you travel far or have to make it expensive, many places are free to visit.

In London, for example, Tate Britain and Modern galleries, British Museum, Natural History and Science Museum, Victoria and Albert, and the Maritime Museum are all free to visit to name a small few.

Most big cities have free attractions, as well as an abundance of history and heritage, telling their story of how life used to be, and is now, for the people that live there.

Turning down a backstreet can reveal something interesting.

When you immerse yourself in another place, where you are at that moment in time, it feels a bit like time stands still, as everyday life carries on around you.

This feeling is the most powerful for me, when I stop and people-watch. I would positively encourage you to stop and do this regularly.

Find a bench, a spot in the park, sit by a river or on a beach, and watch the world go by. Step away from the hustle and bustle of life, and watch it continue around you.

It is fascinating to watch other people and relaxing to sit there without any other distractions.

If you are not used to sitting still or being alone it will take practice to relax.

It is calming, and gives you a moment to think and reflect, taking some precious time out just for you is important.

Look at what surrounds you, breathe deeply and take it in, look at the trees, watch the ducks, the children playing, the sea rolling in, take a sandwich and enjoy everything that is out there just waiting for you to discover.

PART 6

Being Human

Do it now

The impact that you have on others

Friendship

Becoming a parent

The end of a relationship

Dating

Celebrate the good stuff

Being human

The greatness of humanity is not in being human, but in being humane
Mahatma Gandhi

What does it mean to be human?
We use a plethora of adjectives to describe being human, kind, sympathetic, and understanding, as we as a species have the power to articulate speech.

It has been said that being human is simply understanding that others are human too.

But what does being human look like?

About five years ago, I was in a department store walking behind an elderly couple, their progress was quite slow as they were trying to get onto the rising escalator in front of them.

They were holding hands and the elderly gentleman apologised to me for being so slow, he said that he was young once, and they hadn't always been this way.

I was already smiling at them and explained that I was smiling because I found it so touching that they were still holding hands.

He looked at me intensely and said, I have to hold her hand nowadays or she would wander off and I would lose her.

In his eyes the look that passed between us stopped me in my tracks, it was full of pain and fear.

I understood how frightened he was, not for himself, but for his wife, as she was becoming more confused. He didn't need to say any more we both knew how he felt.

The way he looked at me in that moment, conveyed the pain of losing the life they'd had together, the uncertainty surrounding what they were going through, whilst translating his fear of how and when it would all end.

How do we tell someone in this heartbreaking situation that everything will be alright?

We can't, it won't, they will always be hollow words.

The future is forever changing, influenced by the people you love and cherish as they move forward with their life. It might mean big changes for you, depending on the importance of the role they play in your life.

This is a good time to address your own life and your ability to adapt and change. You too can redesign your life.

This experience with the elderly couple has stayed with me, I truly felt that I could see through this gentleman's eyes, and I have thought about the outcome for them countless times.

When I present to groups, I often mention two dead parents being motivating in lots of ways.

This is my dark humour approach to dealing with something that was completely devastating at the time.

Every day I miss something about what might have been, these thoughts are a part of my life but don't dominate it.

A fleeting thought that has an element of sadness or a funny memory, sometimes it's a guilty feeling of not having done enough. I am not sure that you ever feel that you have done enough when you are nursing someone you love dearly towards the end of their life. Watching them deteriorate and helping them on their journey to cease to exist before your very eyes.

The feeling that I should have been a better daughter in some way jumps up sometimes in my head and tries to make me feel inadequate, I address this thought quickly and squash it.

Guilt is not helpful in this scenario, I know rationally that I did the best I could at the time, the last thing my mum would want is for me to live my life feeling terrible.

Sad thoughts sometimes surface, the same narrative usually plays, "if only my children could have met my mum," and thoughts about how much they have missed out on by not knowing her.

How wonderful it would be to be called "my daughter" again.

Would I still be the same person writing this if my experiences had been different?

Probably not, I have accepted my reality and chosen to live my life positively.

We are all shaped by our experiences but don't have to be defined exclusively by them.

I am lucky to have had the role model of my mum.

I always felt loved, and although my childhood was old-fashioned in a lot of ways, it taught me valuable lessons that have helped me in life.

I look back with happy memories, however short, and try to live in a way that would make her proud.

Finding ways through, altering the plan and accepting what is happening, is not easy but it does build resilience and strength.

An acquaintance of my husband had arranged to move house with his wife of over 50 years into a retirement village, a long way from where they previously lived. Having scoured the country for the right location, within a week of signing the papers, just before the move, she suddenly died.

He was obviously devastated, but eventually decided to move anyway and he now has a very different life.

He always had an enthusiasm that is infectious and has successfully managed to redesign his future, adapting to the life-changing situation he found himself in.

The huge loss is still there, present in his thoughts, but he knows his wife would want him to enjoy his life, and he is discovering a new way to live.

How often do we hear of a family tragedy, losing a child, the death of a husband or wife, and the need to make the loss mean something positive often drives amazing things to happen?

Worldwide life-changing charities are set up, and there are thousands of examples of making a difference, helping millions of other people to have a better life as a result of the circumstances and their actions.

Of course, you would always want those cherished people back in a heartbeat, it doesn't make the pain of the loss any less.

But when that isn't going to happen, what huge strength is shown by us humans, to move onward, and make such a difference to others, how proud those people they lost would be.

Great adversity can be a catalyst to make monumental changes to your life, and the life of others, as your focus on what matters becomes crystal clear.

Do it now

Here is the test to find whether your mission on Earth is finished: if you're alive it isn't
Richard Bach

I was 29 when my mum died and having already lost my dad when I was 7, I learnt from an early age that time can be short, and we don't all live to be 100.

I am sure a psychologist would say that this is why I am driven to do lots of things and am regularly trying to fit too much in.

Perhaps it's also why sometimes, I don't live in the moment, as I am busy planning the next adventure so I don't miss out, without being truly present in my life, this would be a fair assessment.

When my mum died, I had the soul-destroying task of clearing out her house.

I walked into the empty house, and it echoed with sadness and loss.

As if it knew that waiting for the occupant to return was pointless, mirroring my feelings of despair and helplessness, it was terrible.

If you have ever had to do this, you will know that nothing can prepare you for how it feels to walk in alone, with no one there to greet you.

One of the things I found extremely sad, was opening the wardrobe and finding her brand new clothes hanging up still with their tags on. And the new shoes at the bottom of the wardrobe, all patiently waiting for that special occasion that never came.

Beautiful things never to be worn, saved for best, like in times past, when the best room in the house was rarely used except for important visitors.

Live your life now, this isn't a rehearsal, and nothing has illustrated this to me more than looking inside that wardrobe.

Wear those clothes, use that perfume, go out to those places, meet those new people, step outside and look at all the things the world has to offer you.

Be excited about your life, and if you are not excited, find something to make this your daily reality.

Each day gives you the chance to start again, when you lose someone close it should teach you how to live, we comment that life is short and then continue to waste it.

Use this sad but powerful lesson to motivate you to really live, and remember that just being alive is the special occasion.

The impact that you have on others

To know even one life has breathed easier because you have lived, this is to have succeeded
Ralph Waldo Emerson

People matter not possessions, this is a direct quote from my late mum, which I have forgotten over the years at various times when my priorities have been in the wrong order.

I recently attended the funeral of a person who used to be a good friend, and when the personal speeches began about his life, it made me think about the impact we have on others.

Not the immediate and obvious effect that you can see and easily measure, the cake you bake, the lift you give, the money you lend, but the influence that you have without knowing it.

I also thought how sad it is, that most of us never tell each other about the impact other people have had on our lives.

It's too late when you are sitting at a funeral listening to a speech like this one.

I met up with a friend again, we knew each other well when our children were young but hadn't seen each other for over ten years.

She started talking about what a difference I made when she had been ill all those years ago.

I had arranged to be the point of contact, to stop everyone from calling her asking for news, it was distressing when she had to keep repeating the same information.

I don't even remember doing this and was surprised that it had made such a difference to her.

Another friend said that when they were dealing with the death of their father sixteen years ago, I was helpful and easy to talk to as I understood and could offer words of comfort.

This was good to hear and made me question the part we all play in the lives of others without realising how important it might be to them.

I think particularly when it comes to the death of a person, people find it uncomfortable or embarrassing to talk about, it is a part of life and has been a part of my life for a very long time now so I don't fear it, when we fear it, we act in all sorts of strange ways.

When my dad died, as I mentioned I was only a child, and no one spoke about it.

I wasn't allowed to go to the funeral, things were dealt with that way then.

I couldn't comprehend what had happened, and why he wasn't talked about at all after his death.

I remember being told by a well-meaning relative who was looking after me at home, as my dad's funeral took place, that I would need to look after my mum now.

I acknowledged this almost unknowingly and carried the burden forward into all aspects of my future relationships.

Never one to shy away from responsibility, it became a big part of who I am.

It took a lot of unpicking, many years later to reach the point of clarity and realisation, that I am not, in any way responsible for everything that happens to everyone I know.

I don't have to fix anything for them or try very hard to make it better, ultimately it is not my responsibility.

I understand now as an adult, that for my mum, the memories of my dad were too painful for her to relive, and she was trying to protect us both from further distress.

This had the opposite effect at the time and left me feeling very hurt, thinking he couldn't have mattered much, or been very loved, as everyone had forgotten him.

With no one to talk to about the way I felt, it became a bit of a shameful secret.

When you can't talk to people about how death is affecting you, it can close you off, and shut a part of you down.

As death is a part of all our lives, we need to find a way to talk about it.

What you say to others can have such a long-term impact on their lives without you realising it.

The impact of what you say to children, positive or negative, encouraging or critical, can change the course of their life.

How sad is it, that the person whose funeral it is will never know how their kind words, deeds and actions, made such a difference in so many people's lives?

The kindness of a stranger as well as kind words from those I know well can make me cry with emotion.

I often have a strong reaction to kindness at times of frustration and desperation, not understanding why this would make me so upset.

I think it is because you have shown your vulnerability, that the reaction of kindness and understanding from others can be overwhelming.

It is uncomfortable to let your inner pain escape, almost preferring someone to shout, so you can keep tight control of everything that is going on inside.

I recently got remarried and my two grown-up sons gave me away, both made a speech, I was hugely proud of them.

It was so emotional, humbling and life-affirming, to hear what they said about me and my new husband.

If we hadn't got married, I don't think I would ever have heard their view of me as their mum, and what I meant to them in their life.

I was surprised by their depth of feeling and their portrayal of who I am, knowing the real me far better than I could have ever imagined.

If you can let those people in your life know how you feel about them and how they have enhanced your life, they will be surprised and delighted and may have something wonderful to say to you too.

The ripple effect of dropping a pebble into a pond is well known, as the pebble lands the circles ripple outwards on the water.

The ripples get bigger and bigger, reaching further and further out, all affecting each other in the same way that your impact radiates out throughout your life.

To end as I began, people matter, not possessions, wise words from my lovely mum, who had such a positive impact on so many people's lives.

Friendship

Friends are the family you choose
Jess C Scott

I spent a lot of years in friendships that were quite damaging to me.

Apparently, you are the average of the 5 friends that you spend the most time with, so choose them carefully.

This shapes who you are, and in this count, friends include your romantic relationships too.

The 5 people you choose should not be by accident, your closest circle should offer you the guidance and support you need and hopefully help to stretch your thinking.

Different viewpoints and opinions will influence the person that you grow into, and this can have both positive and negative effects.

If you spend a lot of time with very negative people this will rub off on you and change your thinking.

In the same way, you will subconsciously start to speak the same language by using the same words and phrases as these people.

Being involved with someone who is very negative is exhausting, if you dread seeing them it's a clear sign that this is not healthy for you.

Make sure you want to be influenced by them, that they are good for you and uplifting.

Do they have your best interests at heart as they will shape your future and help you to dream big or limit your thinking?

Friends come in different varieties, some are superficial friends who want to befriend you for a particular purpose but will never develop into a substantial friendship.

I have been stung by these types of friends in the past, as I misunderstood the friendship was transient, one-sided, and was only valuable to that person when I was in a powerful and influential position.

It is amazing who falls by the wayside when your status changes, another valuable lesson in choosing your friends wisely.

Not all friendships, outside the 5 (and you can have more than 5), need to be deep and meaningful. You will probably have many casual friends on social media and at school or work, with enough in common to enjoy some time together when you are part of the same group or sports team.

True friendships need you both to equally engage, wanting the best for you and having a genuine interest in your life as you have in theirs.

Friendships should be built on trust, respect, and admiration for each other.

They should offer you a safe place to be at your best and your worst with reciprocal support.

You don't have to agree on everything, that would be dull, but have enough respect for each other for it not to matter.

Shiny new friends can offer you a quick fix for the here and now. Like fashion, they can be a passing phase to fit your life at that time, and that's ok, we don't have to keep all our friends forever.

I believe that some are meant to be just passing through to teach us something about ourselves, even if it is something difficult and uncomfortable, it gives us a chance to reset and take stock of who we want to become.

Make sure you put enough value on those true friends you can turn to in times of crisis.

I lost an amazing friend for a few years as I didn't put the effort in and was very distracted with new pursuits, her comment was, "It is easier to get an appointment with the doctor than to get to see you!"

I had neglected my friend when she needed me and I chose unwisely not to put the effort in. I am happy to say we are great friends again now.

There is nothing more rewarding than having a good time with your friends, being comfortable together doing nothing, celebrating and sharing life's highlights, just being there supporting each other at challenging times throughout your lives.

You know when you click with a person, it just feels right, you don't have to work too hard at it, enjoy those true relationships even when shiny new ones come along, and don't forget the old faithful ones.

It is worth getting this right, studies show that you live a happier and less stressed life with strong friendships in place, and their influence and support are more important than even your family.

The skill is to recognise those that are worth keeping, your time is valuable so don't waste it with people you don't want to be with and who make you unhappy, this is your life, so you get to choose.

Becoming a parent

Becoming a parent is like taking a trip to a foreign country, you have no way of knowing beforehand what you'll encounter once you get there
Ann Douglas

My scariest experience ever, bar none, and the biggest and steepest learning curve of my life.

As an avid reader, I was prepared for this, I knew what it meant to be a great parent. I had read all the books, scoffed at those who couldn't control their children and was ready to become the best parent ever.

Newsflash, I knew nothing!

The reality of becoming responsible for another living being was terrifying. Right from the start, trying to work out how to put him in a car seat to even make it home from the hospital to get him in through the front door was hard.

Everything about becoming a new parent screamed to me that I was a fake and an amateur.

Add to this the utter exhaustion of a baby that wouldn't sleep, and within a few weeks, I was in a grim place.

My best friends were now the washing machine, fridge and television, getting out of the house required a lot more planning and preparation than I had the energy for.

On reflection, this is not the time in your life to be polite and say you can manage by trying to do everything yourself.

When you still don't ask for help to save face and you fail to cope well, it's a bad decision that results in other bad decisions, and your life becomes more and more unstuck.

If like me you are thrown off balance into a scary and unpredictable world that you were convinced you'd prepared for, ask for help.

I had people who supported me, but I don't think I ever let on just how daunted I was by this massive life change.

I could not understand how one small being could cause so much chaos and turmoil.

Being in control was a fundamental part of who I was, but the new small person in my life didn't seem to understand this, he hadn't read the manual.

This is the time to be kind to yourself, and realise you are not perfect, and neither are any other first-time parents, despite their well-polished external faces and perfectly manicured nails.

Take it one day at a time or an hour at a time if you need to, and embrace all the non-judgemental help you can get.

Ignore any tips, wise words or advice on how to be the perfect parent when you are informed by other well-meaning parents, how to raise the perfect child their way. If you look at their offspring with a sense of fear and uneasy trepidation they are not the blueprint you need to follow.

As your confidence starts to appear and you get to know your baby, you will find what works for you and you will learn together.

Most of us fall instantly in love with our children and know that they are cuter, smarter, and will progress quicker than any other child out there!

I am joking of course, but it is a good job that nature works in this way as we learn to cope with the lack of sleep and the constant sick and poo parcels that we are presented with.

As this phase ends, the joy continues when they begin to toddle around, and your once safe house now looks like a death trap. It's a regular race to see who can get to that plug socket or hot pan first.

Moving on to when your angel starts to have their own opinions and you realise for the first time, that they don't think like you do, or agree with you on anything, deep breathing helps.

I found each stage, from him growing from a baby to a toddler, starting school, as a challenging teenager through to him leaving home, an experience where I learnt so much, my firstborn was also my training ground as he grew, we both grew.

When he left home at 18, I couldn't believe that part of his life and mine was over, I wanted to start it again, to be better, to get it right this time.

I know now that there is no right, just the best you can do in the circumstances that you are in, and as each child is unique, what works for one child might not work for another.

By the time I got to children number two and three, it was so much easier, like anything you do, with practice you get better at it, thank goodness.

The end of a relationship

And sometimes good things fall apart so better things can fall together
Marilyn Monroe

Accepting that it was finally over and that things would never be the same again was unbelievably hard.

It took a long time for the reality to settle comfortably within me, the reality that my marriage was finally over after 22 years.

Even when things were not right for both of us and we were very unhappy, what was familiar felt like a safer and more comfortable place to be than the alternative.

It was more attractive than it should have been to stay, and fear of my unknown future stalled any change for quite a long time as I tried to imagine a life on my own.

The decision to end a relationship takes courage and it is often about more than just two people, our children were our primary concern, but we couldn't continue no matter how hard we tried.

Fear of the unknown is a limiting factor and stops you from making good decisions.

What will I do?

Where will I go?

Who am I?

These were my questions, and they relate not only to personal relationships but to the end of work relationships as well, both can be devastating.

If you have ever been in this type of situation you will recognise the feeling of the ground suddenly disappearing from under you, looking down and thinking oh, what do I do now?

The who am I question took me by surprise, with hindsight it shouldn't have. But at the time it threw me into turmoil for a while, as my identity was wrapped up as part of a couple for such a long time, it was not just my own.

As a daughter-in-law and sister-in-law, I had other titles that I would lose, not only my wife status, and having lost my parents and with no siblings, this felt like another big loss.

Feeling my way through my new reality and learning how to be me, was eventually exciting but I needed a complete rewrite of the things I thought I knew about myself in the process.

I questioned all my belief systems, if I were a garden, it was like all the plants were still there, but someone had moved them to another place, some had grown much bigger and some had greatly reduced in size.

I use the garden analogy because it makes sense to me.

All the bits that made me were still there, but I had been shaken up and everything had landed somewhere new, bits of me I hadn't seen for years reappeared, blossomed and took centre stage, things that I believed about myself, the things I was very sure of, I began to question.

Also, plants need to be nurtured and cared for and we have to do this for ourselves.

I needed to heal, and being kind to myself nurturing both my mind and body gave me the best chance for my future.

After such a big life change, and mine included the end of my marriage, finding a house to rent and a new job all at once, I began to work out ways to make myself happier.

Acknowledging my new reality, accepting that my path would be a rocky one for a while, whilst working on ways to make positive changes to feel more fulfilled in life began to drive me on.

Fear started to take a back seat as I began to realise what I could do and what I could achieve. I got a glimpse of who I could be, gaining confidence from each new experience.

It is challenging but you need to put yourself out into the big wide world again, congratulate yourself for surviving and find things that will bring you joy and make your heart sing.

Our children were included in almost everything, and I talked a lot with them, as they tried to come to terms with the new versions of their parents as two individuals.

This doesn't mean it was easy, but it was still the right decision for us.

I started to embrace new friends and new challenges, you don't have to like everyone and everything, I didn't, but some things were life changing.

A quest for learning, alongside a childlike excitement for new activities has meant that my life is more fulfilled than I could ever have imagined.

Whether it is the end of a personal relationship through divorce or death or any relationship that has come to an upsetting end, it is awful.

If it is the end of a job through redundancy, retirement, or having to leave for another reason, you will move on if you are prepared to let yourself, it may take a while, but you will.

I worked in two businesses where the end wasn't what I would have wanted it to be.

It is a big shock if it doesn't end on your terms, how or when you thought it would, and frightening if you have no plan in place.

However, after your new reality settles in and the shock begins to fade you will begin to accept the loss.

This allows you to reset, the change may have been forced upon you, but you can choose how you use it to drive you forward to start to design the type of life that you want to live.

I know that the devastation will pass as you start to move on, you have no choice but to accept things in the end, unless you want to live your life stuck reliving the past and that would be a waste of your life.

Dating

Date someone who gives you the same feeling as when you see your food coming at a restaurant
Unknown

It was with interest, hope, and a little trepidation that I joined the world of online dating.

Like many, never expecting to be in this position, I started to learn the rules of the game, and I found that it is a game, where no rules apply.

I consulted with my daughter to inform her of my decision to start internet dating, and to get her to remember my most engaging character traits, so I could use the best version of me for my profile.

I received mixed opinions from my friends about the online dating world, some of whom had vast past experiences to prove that this was not a good idea, but where else could I go to meet anyone?

When I put my photos online, I was selective, trying to strike a balance between fun and carefree, still young enough to gently party, while trying to look interesting, and being capable of easily having an informed debate.

Fortunately, I didn't attract the dreaded photos of genitalia randomly landing on my phone, so the consensus was that I must have got it about right.

I chose which sites I used carefully, without the left or right swiping as my self-esteem couldn't have coped with the constant rejection.

Sites that offered quick gratification weren't for me, I hadn't been naked with anyone new for over 22 years so no chance with a stranger.

I wasn't sure what or who I was looking for, but I was looking for more than one night and ideally wanted some interesting conversation.

So, date number one, well-matched when chatting online, lots of fun, a little bit flirty, and like me, he had children and enjoyed working.

We communicated for about 2 weeks and then arranged to meet up at a local pub, early in the evening just for a drink.

What a kind, genuine and nice man, so not for me.

We had a lot in common and understood each other easily, but there was no spark, and I didn't like his soft voice, he was nice, but I needed more than nice. If I had spoken to him on the phone, I wouldn't have arranged a date, so at least I learnt something, and he got me through the first one and back out there.

Date number two, a gentle artistic and creative soul, who instantly made me want to parent him, he was a little bit lost, but I would not be the one to rescue him.

Onto date number three, and now we reach the dater who sent me a message as I was on my way to meet him stating "break her bed, not her heart," the only reason I turned up was that I had already driven for nearly an hour to get there, so don't judge me.

Date number three had aged considerably from his profile photograph and admitted to providing a rather youthful version.

Peter Pan didn't reappear throughout the evening, although his entire relationship history did, and unsurprisingly the flaws and faults in all his past relationships were never his.

Date number four, the serial dater whose ex-wife was 15 years younger than him and a model, did I mention that? Yes, at least 20 times!

He was still in love with his ex, the most beautiful woman he had ever met.

I genuinely hope he has managed to move on to save other ladies from the experience I had, and stopped serial dating once and for all.

My friends commented that my organised business-like approach of ruling people in and out quickly on the dating sites was typically me, not wanting to waste time, organising and controlling everything.

In my defence, to manage the number of new people and messages bombarding your inbox you do need an effective system to manage it all and I like to control the chaos.

By now I was getting used to the extremes of feelings as you move from the first tentative online conversation to the now next stage of a phone call.

I did reject a gentleman at this stage who still lived with his mother, he had never been outside the city he lived in, rejected partly because of his narrow perspective but mainly because I didn't like the sound of his voice.

It is a cruel, cruel world.

Before meeting in person, I would imagine all possibilities of what the date would be like, moving swiftly between dizzy excitement and feeling sick.

Would I ever meet Mr Happy ever after, or just have fun for a while, and would I ever get to a second date with anyone?

Ultimately, this could be it, they could be the one, did I want a one when life could change forever, and I liked my existing life?

With this type of mantra in my head, it's a wonder I persuaded myself out of the door at all.

So, onto date number five, he had just joined the dating site and only joined because he was waiting for a webinar to start and was bored, he had never been married and had no children.

When we were arranging to meet up, he was a bit vague over the phone and wanted to make it lunchtime, as he was out the night before.

The destination was a shopping centre, and the location was outside Sainsbury's, warning bells should have been ringing at this point.

Thank goodness they didn't, we turned up, took our chances, and are now happily married having been together for over 5 years.

He is still a bit vague, was only arranging it for lunch-time as he likes a good lie-in and chose Sainsbury's for practical reasons as it stands out and is easy to find.

He was the one, no question, no doubt, I knew at once.

Is he perfect in every way?

No, but neither am I, and as we have already discussed there is no perfect.

A successful relationship I believe all comes down to how much compromising you are willing to do, like in business, what are your deal breakers, your non-negotiables?

Are you having to compromise too much of who you are and what you believe to make it work?

How much of you will bloom and be nurtured by this person and can you show them all parts of you, even the parts you don't like sometimes, and can they show you the same?

When you fall in love, all logic and rationale leave through the window for a while as our happy hormones blind us from the reality of spending a lifetime with someone else.

It's a good job that nature helps us out in the beginning, otherwise, I don't think we would ever get together with anyone.

Life will throw each of us tricky situations to negotiate our way through, if your relationship is good, you will have the person by your side who is learning and growing with you throughout your life together.

For the long term though after the wooing stage has passed and you have put your clothes back on, after the initial excitement has faded and your true selves eventually emerge, when you can trump and shout again, you must decide if you are in love with a person that is good for you.

Will they consider your needs, be your cheerleader and be at the front of the queue with love and support, determinedly in it for your long-term future on the unpredictable rollercoaster of your lives?

This doesn't mean they will do what you want all the time, never disagree with you, or have their own opinion and voice it loudly, no matter how annoying this may be.

Celebrate the good stuff

The more you celebrate the good, the more good you discover that is worthy of celebration
Rabbi Sacks

I am sure that celebrating the good stuff sounds simple and why wouldn't you want to do it?

From working with many businesses and from my coaching work, I know that we don't do enough of this. We fail to congratulate ourselves and celebrate with others when we are doing well.

I have found that a lot of businesses focus on what is wrong, what is seen as a weakness, or mistake takes front and centre stage in discussions for far too long.

Continually playing out in boardrooms across the country are the errors, most not monumental, with senior leaders struggling to move on, and the blame game very much in action.

People rarely get it wrong on purpose, and developing this type of culture at work or home creates fear and destroys creativity.

It becomes a habit to look for what is wrong, and the great things that people are doing go unnoticed, as uncomfortable dramas continue to serve no purpose.

In the workplace, great people start to leave as no one values or appreciates them, and it takes a long time for companies to work out why, wasting valuable time and adding cost to the business with every new replacement.

Many parents, and this has included me at times, are very quick to jump on the unacceptable behaviour of their children and all the good things that are happening, the "little victories" in their lives and yours are rarely acknowledged or rewarded.

Who doesn't like to be told "well done that's great", or "thank you for that it helped?"

If the only time a child gets attention is when they do something wrong, a child thinks, why not misbehave, at least I get attention.

If I play quietly nobody notices me and I play alone.

It can be tempting to leave your children to play alone when they are playing quietly to get all the jobs done, and of course, it is necessary for you and your children not to need to be together every minute. But stop and play sometimes, I was always pleased when I did.

If you don't do it when they are little, as they get older, and their games become more online based you will have less opportunity to be involved.

And as they move towards the teenage years with more independence just being together in the same room can be a novelty.

Although in my case we lived quite a distance from all the big shops, and their sporting activities were all over the place, so I managed to have some good conversations with them in the car, as they were trapped with me and had no choice.

Life can be hard, and work and children can be challenging, but surely there must be some good stuff to celebrate and positive things to say.

Reinforcing good things that happen, focusing on the positives and being kind becomes a habit, the more you do it the more natural it feels.

It doesn't take much to make someone's day and make a difference in their life, or to celebrate something in yours.

If you constantly look for the good stuff, you will find green shoots of children and adults trying to do the right thing everywhere, every day.

PART 7

Happiness alone is overrated

Words are like bullets that lodge in your brain

Problem–solving

Confrontation

Stick to your guns

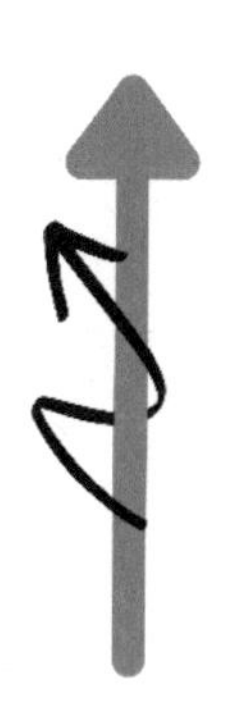

Happiness alone is overrated

I used to think the worst thing in life was to end up all alone, it's not. The worst thing in life is to end up with people that make you feel alone
Robin Williams

The range of emotions that we feel throughout our lives are supposed to be there.
It is normal to feel the full range, whether you are angry, jealous, sad or disappointed, embrace it and work out what feeling this way is trying to tell you.

We cannot be happy all of the time.

All your emotions are useful, if you pay attention to what you are feeling, you can try to work out why you are feeling this way. Then you can question yourself about what you can do to feel differently.

If you are expecting others to do this for you, to change the way you feel, they may succeed sometimes, but this puts a lot of pressure unfairly on them and leaves you waiting around feeling frustrated, as you expect others to fix your emotional state.

Being there to support someone is not the same as expecting them to alter your mood.

In the same way that if you are waiting around hoping someone will change the essence of who they are for you, you are likely to be disappointed.

If you feel angry, what is your inner voice trying to tell you, is it because you fear something new?

This is how I react every time I must do something new on the computer where frustration and fear result in pointless anger.

I try to relax, take a moment, breathe and remind myself that I will figure it out, I have a much better chance if I can remain rational and calm.

Anger is often triggered by what has happened to us in the past, possibly when you felt powerless, and it surfaces as a reminder.

Maybe it is telling you to take control of something this time, and is justified as it helps you to stand up for yourself.

With this type of anger, use the energy it creates to drive you in your life, as long as your response is rational.

If your anger is driven through your belief system, through the immediate fight or flight response we looked at before, take a moment to work out where this comes from.

Are you projecting another situation unfairly onto this one and is your response out of proportion?

If you can identify which type of anger it is when your anger is at a low level, whether it is justified or from your belief system, you will realise that sometimes it is trying to help you.

At other times you are overreacting, knowing this, means you get to choose how you respond.

Jealousy is another powerful emotion and similar to envy, if left unchecked, it will destroy you.

Jealousy is often relationship-based and focuses inwards towards you, based on a desire to protect something that you have as you worry about someone else taking it.

This is not new news, but you can't change what someone else thinks and feels, no matter how hard you try or how much you want them to be with you.

But you can destroy yourself in the process and what might have been a healthy relationship, by catastrophising and imagining all sorts of things happening that are not real, so you push someone away by relentless questioning and your lack of trust.

It says a lot about how you value yourself if constant reassurance from others is the only way to make you feel precious and loved.

If they are treating you appallingly, your inner voice is trying to protect you, showing you the warning signs so you make the right choice to get out of what is destructive for you and causing you pain.

A word of caution, make sure your inner voice is fact-based when you hear it, calm and rational, and does not bring with it the history of every relationship you have ever been in, because that would be your belief system talking again.

The feeling of envy projects outwards, usually wanting what another person has, whether it's money, their status or perhaps the way they look.

Being envious that they have something that you don't has a feeling of unfairness, and it could be that it makes you feel inferior.

When someone wins the lottery, we like to feel that they are good people who have worked hard and deserve it.

If someone wins who we don't deem as worthy, we are less kind and although in both cases they have the money, and we don't, we don't envy them both in the same way.

Somehow, we can settle our envy quicker in the first scenario than in the second, so we are in control of how we react even if it is subconsciously at first.

If someone gets promoted at work and you think it is unfair, maybe it really should have been you. You can use your envy to drive you to ask questions to work out how you can get to that position, what you need to do, or is it time for you to find a position elsewhere.

You are in charge, and although it is hard, you can act and move forward changing your envy into positive action.

This approach will make your envy diminish as you focus on your life and stop craving someone else's.

The alternative is that you choose to let it destroy you, as you dwell in your resentment and unhappiness for the long term, the choice is yours.

Regarding sadness, sad things happen to all of us, it is a part of being alive, as you recognise how you feel you understand that it will pass.

You know from your earlier experiences, when you have felt sad before, you have dealt with it successfully and so you will again, it won't last forever, history tells you that you will cope.

By reaching out to your family and friends you can make sure your sadness is temporary, sharing your feelings and helping each other through it.

This does not include depression, which I mentioned before needs professional help, an identifying sign when it is more than sadness is when the way it affects you is internal and chronic, as I said I felt alone, helpless and very lost.

You have a great advantage when you question and understand where each emotion comes from and why you behave the way you do. It means that you can choose to unburden yourself from the unhelpful traits and confidently choose only positive reactions.

Words are like bullets that lodge in your brain

"It is not the critic who counts; not the man who points out how the strong man stumbles or where the doer of deeds could have done them better. The credit belongs to the man who is actually in the arena, whose face is marred by dust and sweat and blood; who strives valiantly; who errs, who comes short again and again, because there is no effort without error and shortcomings; but who does actually strive to do the deed; who knows great enthusiasms, the great devotions; who spends himself in a worthy cause; who at the best knows, in the end, the triumph of high achievement, and who at the worst, if he fails, at least fails while daring greatly, so that his place shall never be with those cold and timid souls who neither know victory nor defeat."
Theodore Roosevelt

This quote makes me want to get up and get on with it, it shows how the critic should be viewed and leads me nicely onto my next question.

Why do we remember one negative comment in a sea of hundreds of positive ones?

This is something I have struggled with from time to time when well-meaning people have thought it would be good to give me their opinion on something I wasn't asking their opinion on in the first place.

Why do we focus, debate the truth in, and pay attention to hurtful words that often say more about the speaker than the receiver?

If you let yourself enter a circle of self-doubt when hearing harsh words, playing them on repeat in your head, and taking up valuable space, you are raising their status, allowing them to be important, stop it now!

Thoughts that make you question yourself, maybe I am not good enough or perhaps I can't do it after all, are designed to destroy your confidence.

Listening only to harsh words and not absorbing and committing all the positive comments to memory makes no rational sense.

One of my favourite quotes is, "Never accept criticism from someone you wouldn't ask advice from," if you remember this and those you would ask advice from have your best interests at heart, their words should be helpful.

You don't have to like what you are told about yourself in the same way that you don't have to agree with it.

There are supportive and motivating ways to help people to improve and look at their actions and behaviour without destroying their confidence.

Developing and coaching people to be their best includes looking at people's lives and areas that are not so great, the things they want help to work on to change or improve somehow.

This does not include a diatribe of negative comments in the process.

You have to find a way to acknowledge what you have been told about yourself and move on, find a way to convince yourself that one comment will not define how you see yourself and take over your thoughts, ruling and ruining your life.

If, when you think rationally, there may be any truth in the information you are being presented with, use it to do better next time, but remember, just because someone says it, it doesn't mean it's true.

Constantly dwelling on negative words as they land in your brain is madness.

Don't let the words enter your mind for the long term, they will distract you from your real purpose, stealing you away from all the good things you could be thinking and doing.

Balance any negative thoughts with positive statements and put them everywhere.

Have them on your phone, stuck on every mirror in the house, on the fridge, or anywhere that you regularly look, continually reinforcing the positives about you and getting them to land in your brain.

You need to keep feeding the positives to stop the negatives from destroying your confidence and use them to drive out the inner voice of self-doubt.

You are mighty!

Look at everything you have achieved, that day, week, month or year.

When I was going through a particularly difficult period in my life and took far too much notice of the negative comments that were regularly sent my way, I needed to count every positive just to keep moving forward.

From getting out of bed in the morning to making a sandwich it all counts as achieving something, yes, they were small successes for the average person, but at times I didn't think I was capable of anything at all.

Depending on your mental and physical health and where you are in your life, you may be surrounded by mostly positive comments, but it doesn't take much to start to let the odd destructive one in.

Positively thinking about yourself is a good habit to get into and helps to repel the negative comments before they can settle and take root, you need to be the cheerleader in your life.

Problem-solving

The problem isn't the problem. The problem is your attitude about the problem
Captain Jack Sparrow

Firstly, as I have already mentioned, I am a problem solver by nature and that's not easy to live with.

If you are my husband or one of my children who needed a bit of empathy from words I should have used, like "never mind" or "you tried your best" I was unlikely to supply them.

Instead, I would say, "well, if you had done it differently" or "next time to do it better you need to ..." I have discovered this is not easy to live with.

Living with someone who is constantly trying to solve everything, I have learnt, is not always the best way. Often more listening and an understanding comment with empathy would be more welcome.

Could it be that I think I know better or am I just trying to help?

I question myself regularly on this point.

Solving problems successfully in your life, requires a calm review of the situation, taking the emotion out. This is easier said than done, thinking creatively and a little differently is needed for long-term gain.

Reviewing how you got to this point, whether it was partly through your actions or completely accidental, the way forward is the same.

The review process should stop you from repeating the same patterns if you identify your behaviour as part of the cause of the problem. If you are in control of yourself, you can change how you react.

Trying to apply a quick fix will mean the problem, if not properly dealt with, will come bouncing back to you further down the line, remember everything doesn't have to be solved immediately.

Make sure you are dealing with the actual problem, go right back to the root cause, not the spin-offs or symptoms surrounding it, and find out what the core problem is.

Doing the same thing over and over will result in the same outcome, so change your solution if you want to change the outcome.

Pressing pause and sleeping on it will present you with a clearer and more honest picture enabling you to make better decisions.

You need to be flexible and resilient, depending on the problem it might need a lot of effort to think it through, have all the information in front of you, and play out alternative solutions.

Ask yourself -

What would happen if ...?

Until you find the answer that makes the most sense, then you can make a good decision.

Sometimes you need to make a decision that is just for now, you know the decision will change in the future as external factors come into play or when something out of your control happens.

It is never a good idea to react to anything when you are getting angry or overtired as you will regret it, and we know that negative comments said in the heat of the moment take a long time to move on from.

When helping others solve their problems and giving advice generally, it is important to actively listen first and try to take an impartial balanced view as you will often be presented with only one side of a situation.

Sometimes you just need to be the listener and advice is not needed when what action to take has already been decided, no matter what you think or say.

Some problems are huge, affecting your life detrimentally, especially those involving health, money and relationships, and outside specialist help might be the answer.

It is braver to ask for help than to do nothing but keep worrying.

Apparently, over 85% of the things we spend our time worrying about never happen, so we are wasting a lot of time worrying about nothing.

You can make a drama out of the smallest problem if you choose to, maybe you have some friends like this whose problems are quite trivial in the scheme of things.

I know people who thrive on creating a drama, spinning a story, and actively enjoying other people's mis-fortune.

They could easily present a more positive perspective of a situation, but it wouldn't be as shocking or dramatic, avoid the attention seekers if you can. They know that if they offered an alternative outcome they would have to engage in and accept a happy ending, but they are too busy enjoying the drama and their martyr status for this to be a viable option for them.

When people talk about first-world problems it does make me stop and think how important the things that I am worried about or agonising over really are.

Thinking about people throughout the world who are suffering life-threatening problems like the devastating effects of homelessness and starvation helps me to keep myself in check.

That's not to say that solving your problems isn't important, but keep a sense of perspective if you are in danger of becoming very wrapped up in something quite trivial.

I remember complaining to a friend about not having enough time for cleaning my house and her reply was, "At least you have a house to clean, be grateful for it."

You have probably seen the pictorial story of always wanting the next thing, from the first man walking along wishing he could afford to get a bus, to the second man at the bus stop wishing he could afford to buy a bike, to the third man riding the bike wishing he could afford to buy a small car, to the fourth man driving the small car wishing he could afford to get a bigger car, the list of what he wants goes on and on.

This thinking can be applied to most situations in life where we all crave the things that we don't have until we get them, and then we are not satisfied, so we want to get the next thing.

I know the human condition means we all strive for more and better, but I wonder if by always wanting more and more we are creating unnecessary problems for ourselves and others.

Confrontation

If you avoid conflict to keep the peace, you start a war inside yourself
Cheryl Richardson

Confrontation is difficult and making sure that you only deal with facts is important so you can stay in control. Taking the emotion out of a situation, as we have discussed when problem-solving is hard.

This is an especially volatile situation when you are dealing with people with who you have a strong emotional connection as you are familiar with what will trigger the strongest response in each other, and we all know how to use these weapons well.

Confrontation is when the tone of voice used escalates and the situation turns into a more direct attack needing your immediate attention.

This is different from a problem you need to work out how to solve, it is the next level and can be very intimidating.

However, if you don't confront uncomfortable situations and learn how to deal with conflict both at work and at home, you will be continually frustrated, cross and left feeling that everything is out of your control.

I am not suggesting that you challenge everything, but choose your battles, pick those things that are important to you, there are times when the only answer is to confront something head-on when no one is listening to you.

It could be that you are being treated badly at work, and when you try to discuss it, you are brushed off or shouted at.

Maybe you are dealing with a difficult teenager trying to put boundaries in place and they keep moving the goalposts, this one I can relate to.

Perhaps you have an exhausting friend who only calls to tell you about their latest disaster, and you have had enough, or maybe you are being relied upon to do everything for everyone at home, it is ok to make your feelings known, to confront it and stand up for team you.

Find a time when everyone involved is calm, be brave and explain the facts of the situation.

Often people around you won't realise the negative impact this is having on you, and the effect their behaviour is having on your life as you haven't told them.

Ask them for their suggestions as to how they can help you to find solutions and how you can work together to make things better.

It might get heated but that is no reason to give in and concede.

A word of caution, I mentioned the blame game before where everybody loses, allocating blame by reminding people of all the mistakes they made in the past does not help solve anything.

If everyone adopts a defensive stance and doesn't feel safe enough to be openly honest, then try to question how you are all feeling and why, and explore opinions slowly.

Calmly discuss what or who makes you feel this way, giving everyone time to speak.

Seeing things from someone else's point of view is enlightening, even if you disagree, you may find that they are frustrated too but unwilling to confront you.

Take on board what is said and review the feedback, ask yourself if what they are saying is true, even if it is difficult to hear, it should not be a character assassination exercise.

I have had to digest the fact that I won't let anyone help with anything, but then complain loudly when no one does anything.

Similarly, if people at work don't want to help you, or even try to understand how you are feeling, when they should have your welfare as one of their top priorities, then look at working somewhere else or find someone more senior to raise your concerns to.

It is trickier at home, but it's your life, and the people you spend your time with should value you for what you are truly worth, and be willing to confront a few difficult subjects for the benefit of everyone.

Stick to your guns (not actual guns!)

Be yourself, everyone else is already taken
Oscar Wilde

Once you are happy with who you are, what you are achieving and the direction in which your life is heading don't apologise for being you.

How you think is unique, and there is nothing wrong with being strong, proud, and confident.

If you are working to be the best version of yourself and are self-aware, then your views, thoughts, and opinions matter and are just as valid as anyone else's, regardless of your age or background.

I have had discrimination at both ends of the spectrum, from never being good enough in one of my first jobs, which I later learned was all about the female manager concerned, there was nothing I could have done to make her like me and believe me I tried everything.

Through to becoming relatively invisible as a northern middle-aged woman, I don't stand out in a room full of people or annoyingly when trying to get served at a bar.

However, when I start to speak and present about subjects that I am passionate about, I deliver with enthusiasm, experience and knowledge.

I find people are surprised that I do this well as they have prejudged me from my outside shell.

I try to be brilliant and no apology from me is needed to belittle who I am, what I think, or how I look.

Infuriatingly in past work situations, when visiting new clients, the presumption was often made that the junior male colleague I was with, must be in charge until my job title was mentioned.

I am the same person standing there, now acknow-ledged and suddenly elevated to a new status.

On that note, do your homework, if you are meeting people professionally or personally, look them up on social media, find out what they look like, and make sure that you treat them all with equal kindness and respect regardless of their title, and make sure that they treat you the same way.

Sticking to your guns doesn't mean being arrogant, rude or dismissive towards others but it does mean that it is ok to make a stand.

Even if everyone else thinks differently and your views and opinions are unpopular, it is still necessary for you to voice them, being authentic to yourself.

Of course, it can be uncomfortable sometimes, but it will make you feel stronger and build your confidence in the long term.

This takes courage, but finding courage gets easier the more you stand up for yourself and don't compromise on what matters to you.

It is exhausting trying to be someone you don't believe in a lot of the time.

If you are not true to yourself it will lead to frustration and unhappiness in all the areas of your life, whether you are at home, school, university, work, wherever you are, be you, you are enough.

And finally ...

My childhood inspiration

And so, we come to the end of the book

My childhood inspiration

All you need is ...

Something to do
Someone to love
Something to hope for

A little girl with a bonnet on, in a very old-fashioned dress, printed onto a postcard, the girl was called Holly Hobby (apologies if you have no idea who this is, you can look her up), she was my very first inspirational quote and stared at me from my bedroom wall throughout my childhood years.

This was well before quotes were fashionable and a long time before mobile phones and the internet had been invented.

To set the scene a little further, we were excited when Channel 4 launched giving us four TV channels to choose from, and the only takeaway within a 10-mile radius of my house was fish and chips and you had to pick it up.

I digress, but this message not only works brilliantly for my power of three, but it also works well for everyone, everywhere as the basis for a fulfilling life.

How you measure this and decide when you have successfully achieved it in your life is up to you.

A simple hope and dream, with no further explanation needed, it seems so straightforward when boiled down to just three lines.

These three things are what I have now in my life, and I hope that you have them or work towards finding them in yours.

Find quotes that inspire you, write them in this book, or put them on your phone, and make sure you regularly look at them, keep inspiring yourself.

And so, we come to the end of the book

A few options here – Well 3 ...

Put it on a bookshelf and maybe read it again.

Keep writing in it what you want out of life, the changes you want to make, and your successes and use it to regularly review where you are with your life plan.

Pass it to a friend who might also like to read it and encourage each other to live life well.

Is my life perfect now?

No, of course not, but I know the power we all have to shape and change our futures, to confidently direct ourselves in our own lives.

What has gone before, you should learn from, everything that has happened in your life has led you to this point.

I am excited about the next part of my journey, and I hope that you are excited about yours too.

Embrace the changes throughout your life, learn to cope with the bad stuff, celebrate the good stuff, find some joy in the days in between, and remember, it's your one and only life so make your plan and ***Live Life Your Way***.

THINGS I WANT TO REMEMBER ...

If you can dream it, you can do it
Walt Disney

THINGS I WANT TO REMEMBER ...

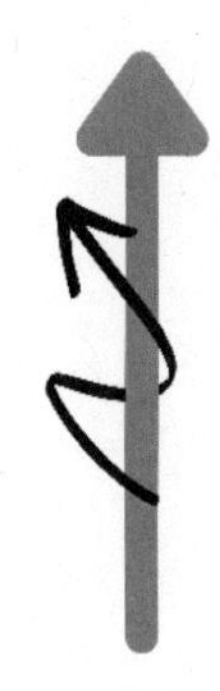

Your struggle in the present is your fuel for your future
Unknown

THINGS I WANT TO REMEMBER ...

I have so much of you in my heart
John Keats

THINGS I WANT TO REMEMBER ...

An adventure was going to happen ...
Winnie The Pooh

THINGS I WANT TO REMEMBER ...

Live Life Your Way
Sally Measom

Acknowledgements

Thank you to my children Daniel, James and Sophie Wake, who have taught me far more than I have ever taught them.

My husband Craig Measom for his understanding and patience, and previously undiscovered proof reading and illustrations skills, I know how much you loved helping me with, "that bloody book!"

Jo Ferguson my oldest friend, it's nearly 50 years and we've shared so much joy and pain in our lives, you're amazing cakes always make things better.

Lisa Harris my friend for over 20 years your humour, opinions and insight are invaluable to me.

Gill Duckworth, Suzanne Stokes and Alice Millard my excellent running counsellors and Fiona DeMowbray my giddy swimmy friend. Tina Gothard the artist, for letting me play art with her.

Eileen and Roger Wake for many adventures together with the children, and Alisia Angel for our helpful chats, I learnt a lot.

Nicki Allsopp and Mandy Elton for befriending a northerner from my time in the south, and Sharon McWilliams and Vanessa Jackson from the S17 years when our children were young.

Tom Rumboll, for picking the wildcard and Steph McGinty and Sue Patterson for being my constant cheerleaders.

Acknowledgements [cont]

Mr H (David Hardman) my first mentor, you changed my thinking and will always be Mr H to me.

Tamsin and James Gilbert our first couple friends, Jane and Tony Phillips and Judy Corble for your support.

Matthew Bird for typesetting and great book advice, and Steve Wake for my websites.

Belinda Huckle and Gavin Keeble from SecondNature, the business presentation skills experts, for providing my next adventure.

www.secondnatureuk.co.uk

Company Shop Group, environmental food surplus experts, I learnt a lot from everyone.

www.companyshopgroup.co.uk

Chatsworth for continuing to inspire me, it's one of my happy places.

www.chatsworth.org

Andy Cope at Art of Brilliance, changing the world one person at a time.

www.artofbrilliance.co.uk

All at Write That Book Masterclass 2022, my group #bestsellers who supported me to get the book finished and Michael Heppell himself whose creative madness and positivity spurred me onwards.

www.writethatbook.co.uk

Acknowledgements [cont]

And Dawn French for inspiration and 30 million minutes.

Finally, a big thank you to you the reader, for picking my book off the shelf and choosing to read it, I hope you enjoyed it and it drives positive changes in your life.

You have all made a difference and I am truly grateful.

Thank you.

About the author

I was born in 1968 in Sheffield, South Yorkshire and spent the first 11 years there before moving to Derbyshire.

I now live in the beautiful Peak District, close to the home of the Bakewell pudding and a stone's throw from Chatsworth House.

Developing people and helping them in their lives is what gets me out of bed in the morning, watching them learn, change and grow is a privilege.

I have three children, one divorce, one new husband, and two dead parents and have had countless house moves and job changes, experiences that have all been translated into this book.

This is my first book, and I am proud that I can now finally call myself a writer having started writing seriously four years ago, it is a label I want to own.

My websites:

www.livelifeyourway.co.uk

www.onehappyplace.co.uk

www.solution3.co.uk